Doing Anger Differently

Helping Adolescent Boys

Michael Currie

MELBOURNE UNIVERSITY PRESS
An imprint of Melbourne University Publishing Limited
187 Grattan Street, Carlton, Victoria 3053, Australia
mup-info@unimelb.edu.au
www.mup.com.au

First published 2008
Reprinted 2008
Text © Michael Currie, 2008
Design and typography © Melbourne University Publishing Ltd 2008

This book is copyright. Apart from any use permitted under the *Copyright Act 1968* and subsequent amendments, no part may be reproduced, stored in a retrieval system or transmitted by any means or process whatsoever without the prior written permission of the publishers.

Every attempt has been made to locate the copyright holders for material quoted in this book. Any person or organisation that may have been overlooked or misattributed may contact the publisher.

Text design by Nada Backovic
Cover design by Nada Backovic
Typeset by Megan Ellis
Printed by Griffin Press, SA

National Library of Australia Cataloguing-in-Publication entry

Currie, Michael.
    Doing anger differently: helping adolescent boys.

    Bibliography.
    Includes index.
    ISBN 9780522854763 (pbk.).

    1. Anger—Case studies. 2. Aggressiveness in adolescence—Case studies. 3. Parenting. 4. Parent and child. I. Title.

152.47

CONTENTS

Acknowledgements	vii
Introduction	ix
When is Anger a Problem?	xvi

PART I THE PROBLEM: ANGER, AGGRESSION AND THE FAMILY — 1

1. The Nature of Anger — 5

Feeling: A Problem or a Sign	5
The Essentials of Anger	7
All the World's a Problem	8
The Relation between Thought and Affect	9
Anger and Ambivalence	11
Anger and Relationships	12
I'll Do What I like	17
The Persecuted Victim	19
Raising Problems with Angry Adolescents	20
In Brief	21

2. Aggression, Anger and Ethics — 23

Sub-types of Aggression	24
Anger, Aggression and Ethics	26
Enhancing Ethics	31
Pro-social, Anti-social	34
The Ethics of Self-interest	36
Self-interest and Self-destructiveness	37
The Certainty of Anger and Aggression	39
Morals and the Social Group	40
Aggression and 'Conscience'	42
Ethics and Rules in Adolescence	44

Adolescence and 'Doing–Being'	46
In Brief	49

3. The Family: Love, Hate and Anger — 51
Douglas's Lost Adolescence	52
Parents	59
The Function of a Father	67
The Child's Internal Family	68
Parental Responses	69
The Guarantee of Parental Failure	74
In Brief	74

4. The Age of Adolescence — 77
Adolescence as a Developmental Turning Point	78
The Overlapping Spheres of Influence in Adolescence	79
Fathers and Alternate Fathers—'Godfathers'	89
Thought, Identity and Morality in Adolescence: Trying It On	92
Adolescent Boys	100
Authority, Tolerance and Limits: The Politics of Rules	104
Certainty and Doubt with Angry Adolescents	105
Resilience in Adolescence	106
In Brief	107

PART II DOING ANGER DIFFERENTLY: TECHNIQUES AND PRINCIPLES — 109

5. The Cycle of Identity: Reaction, Reflection, Action — 117
'Doing–Being' and the Acquisition of Knowledge in Adolescence	118
Being the Parent of an Adolescent	119
Three 'Antidotes to Anger'	120

The 'Cycle of Identity' in Adolescence	124
Following the Cycle	141
How Does this Model Help?	143
In Brief	146

6. What Parents Can Do: Techniques for Intervening with an Angry Adolescent — 148

Constructive Conflict: Turning Crises into Questions	149
Constructive Conflict: A Summary	157
Constructive Contemplation: Helping a Boy Reflect on Anger	159
Constructive Contemplation: A Summary	164
Making Peace: Reading the Signs	167
Cutting Across the Imaginary Contagion and Escalation of Anger	169
Identifying Crises of Possibility	170
Paths to Maturity: Making Plans	172

7. What Adults Can Do: Principles for Intervening with an Adolescent — 173

Using Antidotes to Anger	174
Showing As Well As Telling	176
Knowing What a Boy Wants	179
Constant Presence Rather Than Intermittent	180
Listen To and Notice Your Son	181
The Problem of Lecturing	182
Recognising 'Acting Out'	183
Recognising Differences	184
Affection and Intimacy	184
Rules and Limits	186
Parents Working Together	191
Forbidding	192

The Restructuring of Enjoyment	193
Doubt Revisited	194
Too Much Talk	195

8. Intervening with the School — 196

Investigating the Problem: Approaching the Adolescent	201
Investigating the Problem: Approaching the School	202
Parents Taking Action	203
Teachers Taking Action with Aggressive Students	204
Taking Action: Helping a Student Teach the Teacher	208
Implementing a Plan for Improving School Behaviour	210
Further Points	210
Taking Action: If an Adolescent has Fallen In with the 'Wrong Crowd'	211
Doing Something About Anger and Violence Problems at School	214

Appendix — 219

Further Help	219
Decoding the Helping Professions: Different Types of Professionals	221
Public or Private?	222

Notes — 225
Index — 229

ACKNOWLEDGEMENTS

Associate Professor Wayne Reid, Dr Karen Drysdale and the Hunter Institute for Mental Health for help at the start. Their gifts of recognition of my initial ideas have not being underestimated.

Staff from Creative Times–Reconnect Newcastle, particularly Lauren Graham and Tim Hawes, were especially tolerant and facilitative during the early and often haphazard introduction of my ideas.

Louise Carr, Janine Baker, Anne Kempton and Shelley Williams all gave valuable clinical, material, financial or practical help.

Staff from many schools too numerous to mention aided me enormously by accepting me into their schools and facilitating the construction of an environment where my ideas had a possibility of working. In no particular order, these people include Ollie Mayweld, Peter Morgan, Brett Lambkin, Ron Besoff, Cathy Evans, Julie Myers, Peter Conroy and Paul Sidebottom.

Boys from many schools took risks by participating fully in the program and taught me much. The knowledge is on their side, although at times they did not know it.

Staff at Menslink, particularly Russ Whitehead and Richard Shanahan, took an interest in the program and worked hard at implementing it.

My colleagues and friends at the Centre for Psychotherapy were helpful in taking an interest or encouraging me in my ideas,

Acknowledgements

particularly Susan Burgoyne, Howard Johnson, Chris Willcox, Leonie Funk and also Nick Bendit, who read an early draft of an article and gave helpful comments. Associate Professor Leslie Pollock was helpful in allowing me some time and space to write.

Professor Mike Startup was indispensable for helping me refine my ideas and place them into acceptable forms of analysis at the University of Newcastle.

Colleagues and friends at the Freudian School of Melbourne and the Lacanian Seminar of Newcastle all helped, often unknowingly, in the development of many of my ideas in this book, through their insightful critiques and discussion of presentations I gave in seminars in Melbourne and Newcastle.

Helen Garner kept the idea of this manuscript alive. Hilary McPhee recognised the possibility of the book. At Melbourne University Publishing, Sybil Nolan, Louise Adler and Foong Ling Kong helped in the development of the ideas. Clare Coney's intelligent and detailed editing eliminated the excesses of my text and improved the book substantially.

Most special thanks to Karen and my two girls, Ida and Yvonne, for being there through the whole process.

INTRODUCTION

Tania arrived home a little late from work to find her 13-year-old son, Charles, engrossed in his Xbox game. It was 5.30 p.m. and he should have started his homework.

'Charles, turn off the Xbox!'

Unusual. No answer. Tania put her bags down in the kitchen. She said again, in a not-unfriendly manner: 'Charlie, what about that assignment due in two days!' Tania moved towards the lounge room, from where she could hear electronic simulated gunfire. That stupid shoot 'em up game again!

Tania, quietly: 'Charles! Pause the game, or I will. Charles!'

'Yeah, nearly finished this level, Mum', he replied breathlessly. Tania stepped over and pushed the pause button.

'Oh, Mum! I've just killed three in a row, I'm on a real roll, and I'm nearly getting to the end of the level. Robbie told me when I get to this brick wall I'm nearly there!'

As Tania stepped back her foot caught the power cord, which pulled out of the socket and the screen went blank. 'Oh, Mum! Look at that! I've spent three weeks working really hard to get to this level'—Charles's voice was rising—'and you've just gone and ruined it all! I can't believe it. All because of a stupid assignment that I can do in one hour anyway. Why can't

Introduction

> you just let me enjoy myself for once? If you'd just leave me alone everything would be okay!' Charles stood up and went to his room, slamming the door.
>
> During Charles's tirade, Tania had tried to get out several phrases, including 'You should be doing your homework', 'I don't care about your game', but her words were completely drowned by Charles's surprisingly, almost shockingly loud voice. Part of what was shocking—she kept forgetting this—was how Charles rose more than a foot over her when he stood up while he was yelling at her.
>
> In the stillness after the door slammed Tania felt angry and sad, as well as defeated. How dare her son talk to her like that! Over a ridiculous video game! Why was he getting so angry? Was there something more to this? Perhaps it wasn't just about the video game, which he seemed to use as a means of blocking out the world. What could be wrong? It seemed there was no way around her son's defiance to find an answer to these questions.

The above is a familiar scene to many families with adolescent boys. One of the most difficult problems confronting the parents of an angry, troubled adolescent is that the adults can see that their son is in difficulty, but the boy will not accept the help that parents offer. In exasperation, many parents stop offering help. In this book, I offer ways around this impasse. What parents do during these times of crisis, and what parents say about the situation afterwards, can be crucial in influencing the trajectory of the problem.

However, right at the point of ceasing to help, parents also worry that their son's self-destructive and aggressive behaviour is a sign there is something fundamentally wrong with him. This in itself can be an impediment to positive action, as parents may then seek to explain their son's behaviour in a number of ways.

Introduction

One explanation is that the son's aggression is the result of failed nurturing—that the parents have failed their son somehow during his early years, and damaged him irreparably. Following this line of reasoning, the son's problems are the parents' responsibility—something was wrong with the environment that the parents created when their son was an infant or child. A troubling implication of this logic is that the parent, feeling responsible for the troubles expressed by the teenager, remains responsible, by default, even when the teenager becomes an adult. And however true it may be that a teenager is expressing problems that have their source in childhood, such explanations, transmitted to the child through the family romance, risk detaining the teenager within the position of child. It is as if the teenager has received the message: 'There is little that can be done about your problems—it is your parents' responsibility.'

Alternatively, some parents take up a 'nature' argument. An increasingly popular explanation is that a boy's problems are the expression of a genetic history: figures from the past (often a boy's more or less absent father) are seen as sources of the genetic material of the son's problems. This argument has been given support in recent decades by the increase in diagnosis of teenage problems within a series of psychiatric disorders, which themselves are linked to a genetic heritage, for example, 'I think his father (or uncle) had ADHD'.

The difficulty with these explanations, seductive though they may be, is that they leave little room for the son or the parents to do anything about his present difficulties if the causes belong to the past or to a genetic heritage.

Psychology, psychiatry and the rest of the helping professions have become experts at recognising pathology, destructiveness and abnormal behaviour. Families can become enmeshed in psychological or psychiatric explanations of the 'disorders' from which the son apparently suffers. It is not uncommon for parents to be swept into

Introduction

an ongoing round of appointments that may be more or less helpful but appointments alone are not a solution, unless the teenager and his family recognise that only they can make changes that will solve the difficulties—they are the agents of change in the situation.

Many adolescents, by the fact of their age, are marvellous inventors and improvisers. Their solutions to problems may not fit into the norms provided by psychiatry, but may work very well for the individual boy and his family. Parents, by listening to their sons, can help them recognise and make use of their sons' own inventions.

The 'anger management' movement has been successful in identifying anger as a problem that can be treated. But reducing the solution to anger to a series of relaxation and 'self-talk' techniques, although useful for some boys, ignores core aspects of adolescent anger. His anger is an emotion that inevitably implicates those around the boy: anger is 'caused' by others in his immediate environment. This prevents a boy focusing on what he can do for himself.

A third explanation is that the problems a teenager is experiencing are merely an expression of the developmental stage of adolescence and nothing can be done about them. In my opinion, the so-called 'developmental tasks of adolescence' are a myth that are of little help with individual problems.

Something *can* be done about teenage anger and aggression—and in families where a teenage boy's behaviour is disrupting the family, is aggressive enough to distress other people, and is leading the boy into trouble at school as well as home, something *should* be done. Parents *can make a difference* to their son's behaviour. This book aims to assist parents to understand their adolescent child, rather than measure him against an unreal norm. The book also explains how a boy negotiates the demands of adolescence—which may be in part an expression of how he has subjectively experienced his childhood.

Adolescents are seemingly deaf to reason, yet they assume adult-like qualities as the months go past. Many parents retreat from the

Introduction

battlefield, hoping that they and their son finish his adolescence without too many life-altering injuries. However, problems with anger and aggression, though noticeable in childhood, often become more intense during adolescence, to a point where parents cannot ignore the situation. Problems with angry boys may surface at school or in the home. Parents, teachers, youth workers, foster parents, mentors and others who deal with adolescents who are angry on occasion can do something to help such boys make more constructive use of their anger, or at least direct their aggression in a less self-destructive manner. This is in contrast to a closing-off from family, and the adolescent's striving for dominance and control that often results in fiery, and sometimes violent and aggressive exchanges between the boy and his family, teachers and peers.

It can be difficult to recognise a boy's creative efforts towards self-determination. This book aims to help parents assist their adolescent sons to make meaning of their world, to engage in relationships with those around them and face the difficult transitions that are demanded of adolescents. Anger is a common response—albeit an often ineffective one—of teenage boys to the confusion of growing up. Anger is both a natural ally and deforming monster of adolescence. Anger helps many boys overcome and burst out of the constricting parental limitations of their childhood as they begin to envision and create an independent life. But anger can also create an unnecessary dependence on others to act on past wrongs, and is thus antithetical to the 'I'll do it myself', forward-looking inclination of a more or less healthy male adolescence. Wherever an adolescent boy falls into this spectrum of anger and aggression, adults can help the boy's transition from childhood to adulthood.

This book will allow parents, teachers and other adults to reach out to an angry, troubled adolescent who is bristling with defences that can be set off at any moment. However, helping a teenager cannot be achieved without considerable effort on the adult's part.

Introduction

I do not suggest any quick fixes or magical techniques that will result in an adolescent's anger evaporating overnight. Rather, I advocate a sustained effort over a number of months, even years, which can result in quite severe difficulties with anger and aggression having a surprisingly positive outcome—one that could not be expected given the darkness and depths of an adolescent's rage. This effort can be sustained by an adult's understanding of the nature of anger and its genesis, by taking an authoritative but not authoritarian stance, by drawing out the knowledge implicit in the boy's speech, and by intervening where necessary following a set of principles rather than rigid rules.

To this end the book is organised in two sections. Part I deals with the general nature of anger and aggression and the genesis and expression of these in home and school contexts. It should help adults to recognise the extent of the problem, and gain some insight into the reasons behind it. It explains the thinking that boys go through when they have damaged or destroyed many important relationships, having been labelled as 'troublemakers' or 'angry, aggressive'. Part I finishes with a discussion of the phases of adolescence that are relevant to the expression of anger and aggression and outlines a stance parents can take to shift the boy from a 'paranoid' to a 'critical' habit of mind. I argue that this shift is more or less a matter of how the adolescent makes meaning of his world, which is itself partially a product of what sense he makes of his family life. I also discuss how to make use of the developing knowledge and identity of adolescence, as well as the problems and strengths of an adolescent's friendship group.

Part II outlines in detail the stance of intellectual midwife—assisting with giving birth to new ideas—that adults may take with angry adolescents. This approach can be thought of as an 'emotions coach', where the adult assists a boy to take a different stance in regard to his emotional life.

Introduction

Part II will be helpful to those seeking a general framework for thinking about and changing their relationship with an adolescent, be they parent, teacher, youth worker or adult friend. It gives you techniques—Doing Anger Differently—to reach out to the boy and allow him to change his behaviour. It is important to grasp that you cannot change it for him, he must come to an understanding that it is in *his* best interests to change his behaviour. Chapter 6 deals with more practical issues, and discusses in a focused way what parents can do at times of crisis, to calm and help their son in a constructive manner. Chapter 7 outlines some general principles to guide interventions both at home and at school, and Chapter 8 covers school interventions that parents, teachers and other involved adults can make. An Appendix also covers further avenues for professional help for the adolescent, if needed.

Throughout the book I have made extensive use of case material to illustrate or introduce the points being discussed. I have done so because I have found that people understand best through others' stories, which is the first step (by no means the last) to applying the understanding to one's personal situation. The examples in this book have been altered substantially so that no individuals are identifiable. However, I have retained the general themes, drawn from many years of work with adolescents and their families, and I expect that readers may recognise themselves in the issues with which the individuals of the book are struggling.

The two parts of the book can be read alone or in sequence, according to the reader's interests and desires. The book will be most helpful, of course, if time is taken to read it from cover to cover, as this will allow the reader to understand the general problem, the principles of the Doing Anger Differently approach, as well as specific techniques that parents can use in their interactions with their sons.

Introduction

When is Anger a Problem?

The question of when anger and aggression in adolescence are problems is important, but is hard to answer. Many parents and those dealing with boys may be happy to see the problem as an adolescent one, and attempt to 'ride out' the difficulties in the hope that relief will come at the other end of adolescence and the boy will grow into a respectable, law-abiding, successful adult.

Other parents may attempt to intervene to solve the problem. However, the parent may find that the intervention at best has no effect or seems to make the problem worse. This book can help parents to intervene with the adolescent's view of the world in mind, while not diminishing the problems that anger and aggression cause for the son and those around him.

Perhaps the first question to ask when attempting to determine whether anger and aggression are a problem is 'A problem for whom?'. The fundamental tendency in anger is to see the rest of the world as the problem. For now the angry adolescent may see anger and aggression as useful solutions to all of the problems people are causing for him. When is it time for the other family members, schoolfriends, teachers or others to say that there is a problem?

Ongoing hostility

Generally, if you spot a tendency in an adolescent to regard others around him as hostile when there appears to be little basis for this belief, it is a reasonable indicator that there is a problem. We all have times when we are fearful of the world and feel that others have bad intentions towards us, but if this is an ongoing theme with an adolescent, it may be time to do something about it. This is because such an attitude will result in an adolescent having a lot of difficulty keeping and maintaining friendships. Those friendships he does make will mostly be with others who share a similarly negative and malevolent view of the world around them.

Introduction

Over-reaction and destructiveness
Similarly, when a boy commonly reacts to small slights in a manner that is overly aggressive or violent, this is an indication that there is a problem. In addition, where there may be reasonable provocation, but the response seems out of proportion, the adolescent may need help. If there appears to be a more or less random swinging between attacks on others and seemingly self-destructive acts, it may also be a sign that there is a problem.

Home problems
At home, if a parent finds that he or she is being repeatedly involved in arguments and is worried about the clashes, then there is a problem, at least from the parent's viewpoint. Again, the son may not see this as a problem—he probably views it as the parent's problem and not his. It is easy to infer that Charles saw his mother Tania as the problem—she wouldn't leave him alone. Tania, however, was responding to what she saw as a deeper problem: Charles's avoidance of schoolwork and his increasing isolation. The parent finds him- or herself in the position of arguing for something in the adolescent's best interest that the adolescent does not accept.

If there are repeated heated exchanges at home between parents and their son, and with other family members, then this is stressful and lowers the quality of life for all the family. If approached in the right way and at a cooler moment, then the son will also probably acknowledge that there is a problem.

Likewise, if there is repeated fighting in the house amongst siblings, then this is a problem, most likely for the whole family. These types of problems are discussed in more detail in Chapter 3. Such conflicts may be a reflection of the particular family's style of communicating. Some families use conflict in order to forge connections with each other. This may not seem optimal, even appearing counter-productive to the detached observer. However, conflict can be a manner of changing, maintaining or re-inventing familial relationships. In addition, outright conflict is not in itself necessarily a problem. Open and honest expression of points of view may be an important formative factor for adolescents, and the increase in assertiveness on the part of an adolescent may simply be an expression of his inclination towards mastery that is a natural part of puberty. As outlined in Chapter 4, this inclination towards mastery has its limits, and one of the skills in parenting adolescents generally is knowing how and when to point to and impose limits.

In the case of fighting amongst siblings, attacks on siblings may not make sense, or the apparent reasons for the attack may not be the whole story. Commonly, problems at school are expressed at home and problems at home are expressed at school. Anger and aggression are *opportunistic* emotions and acts, and are most commonly *displaced* from their source. It is important for this reason to not only respond to the situation of anger in the family (i.e., by imposing limits on the adolescent), but also to 'stay in touch' and speak with an adolescent more broadly about how he is going outside the family.

School problems

If parents are receiving reports from school regarding a son's behaviour, this is a preliminary sign of a problem requiring investigation. If the school views the son's behaviour as a problem, then there is a problem for the son, as it has the potential to affect his studies and his long-term life opportunities. However, the son may not acknowledge any problem, as he may believe he is acting in the only manner that he can.

Methods for approaching an angry adolescent, the school and discussing the problem are outlined in Chapter 8. Briefly, it is important not to remain closed to either the adolescent's or the school's viewpoints. Teachers have exposure to the entire range of human behaviour through the students who attend school. If an adolescent is being picked up on the school's radar, it may be a sign that the behaviour-management system set up by the school—which works for the vast majority of students—is not working for the angry boy for some reason. Whilst the school's reports are not a foolproof indicator, they are often a reasonable one deserving attention. Early intervention is important, so that resentments do not build up between the boy and the school.

Peer problems

One important factor controlling aggression is the type of friends that your son spends time with. The single best predictor of negative life outcomes—such as involvement in criminal activity, poor educational outcomes and unemployment—is involvement in groups of friends who also feel rejected and marginalised at school. It is known that such boys form sub-groups which can be involved in aggressive and destructive acts that are valued by the sub-group but ultimately are destructive of a boy's life opportunities. These groups tend to increase a boy's sense of victim-hood in regard to mainstream schooling, and strengthen and consolidate a vengeful 'poor-me' view of the world, with little respect for societal norms. Membership of such groups also tends to make an aggressive adolescent feel better about himself, as his peers congratulate him on his latest destructive act. This problem is dealt with more fully in Chapters 4 and 8, but the simple point now is that parents should know about their son's friendships and who he spends time with. Parents have a right and a responsibility to know where he is.

PART I

The Problem: Anger, Aggression and the Family

Anger is a temporary madness.

Seneca, *De Ira*, circa 40–50 AD

Angry people are not generally considered to be mad, in the sense of having lost touch with social reality, as this is not true when they are not angry. But when we are confronted with an angry person, we perceive the constraints that assure us that the person participates in the social world—just as we do—seem to have fallen away. The angered person appears unpredictable and erratic. We are uncertain of what he or she may do next. Depending on our own emotional fortitude, and what constraints we are prepared to labour under, another's anger can inspire in us a similar 'madness of the victim', or else a passive accommodation of the angry person's wishes—if we can guess how we have aggrieved the angered one. In a family context, such responses lead to a certain madness in the household as well: either a household of people who are intermittently mad and maddening, or adults who find themselves doing all sorts of mad things to accommodate their son, lest he become angry.

The streak of madness inherent in anger has many parents wondering what sort of boy they have produced and what sort of man he will become. Beyond the obvious traumatic impact on the family, if a boy's cycle of sullen withdrawal and explosive anger continues, how will he cope with the world as an adult? Once parents have understood the repetitive nature of the problem, and have been able to put aside for the moment their protest of 'I can't stand this anymore!', many also begin to wonder about the nature of the difficulties. Questions arise such as: 'Is this what adolescence is?', 'Does my son have some sort of psychological problem?', 'What is my part in these difficulties?' and 'What can I do to help my son?' The following chapters attempt to answer some of these questions, while Part II contains a practical program to follow to help the boy.

1
The Nature of Anger

Anger is one possible response where there is 'already a difficult evil present' in the mind; anger is the movement of attack against the evil. To succumb to the evil is sadness. The removal of that evil is both a move towards goodness and a dissipation of anger.

St Thomas Aquinas, *Summa Theologiae*, 1265–73

In my work as a family therapist, mothers (and occasionally fathers) would bring their adolescent sons to see me. The mother would often complain that whilst he was still her son, he had grown up suddenly to be taller, bigger, louder and certainly not as obedient, loving and close as he used to be. Some mothers said they had begun to feel scared of their son at times, particularly when he raised his voice, became agitated, or perhaps started to hit things. Mothers would also complain that their sons retreated, giving monosyllabic answers until the next outburst. This left little opportunity to resolve matters. The meeting with me was an attempt to find a way out of this exhausting circle.

Feeling: A Problem or a Sign?

Answers to the questions posed by parents are unlikely to be found within either the reports of problems at school or the disruptive outbursts that puncture family life with an angry adolescent boy. Many parents find their son has a body that is fast becoming that of a man; however, his emotional life is still at times childlike. There is yelling, slamming doors, the fear of what this boy–man might be capable of in his rage, and anger and resentment in the rest of the family. The outbursts can take on a terrible, monotonous regularity and uniformity. In speaking to school staff and other parents, many find similarities in the angry outbursts. It all leads to one conclusion: if the boy could just control his temper, everything would be fine.

Our tendency to seek answers in the similarities we share with others can lead to the belief that anger is the problem and the son simply needs to stop being angry. However, this is to ignore the fact that anger is a response to something, although it is often unclear precisely what 'it' is. 'It' may not even be what the adolescent says it is.

To blame the adolescent for his angry outburst often only serves to heighten the problem, making him even angrier and more prone to outrage. If parents take on such a 'madness of the victim' approach, things are unlikely to improve and likely to worsen. A sense of persecution may take over other members of the house and little gets discussed or resolved amongst the accusations of wrongdoing. Responding angrily is understandable, often inescapable, but rarely solves the problem, although the angry scene may be an important prelude to a solution to the problem in some families (Chapter 6 discusses this further).

The uniformity of the angry outburst that I discussed above is deceptive. There are myriad individual causes that underlie the emotion of anger. A central theme of this book is that the solution to problems with anger and aggression lies in assisting adolescents to reflect on *what it is* that disturbs them to anger, rather than simple 'anger management'.

The Essentials of Anger

Anger is an emotion that involves two notions. First, a perception of some wrong, or problem in the world, committed by someone else, and second, a sense of the unfairness or the injustice of this wrong. Anger is a sign of a mismatch between what a boy wants (or at least what he knows he doesn't want), and how he perceives the world to be. Simply, the square pegs of the son's wishes do not fit into the round holes of the world around him, created—it seems to him—by parents, siblings, teachers and peers.

It should not be forgotten that anger can be a productive response to a difficult situation, as the epigram to this chapter reminds us. Although Aquinas places the problem elsewhere, an adolescent's complaint against others contains the seeds of his own wish, in the 'difficult evil' present in his mind. Anger may be an important factor in overcoming the reluctance to say what in fact 'needs to be said', thus revealing the 'difficult evil', which can then be spoken about. Anger can be a preferable reaction to sadness, which hides by rendering internal the 'evils' that an individual bears. Being angry can allow one to feel more capable and in control. For many boys anger is a psychically protective emotion when responding to difficult or threatening situations, and the complaint against others may be the only way a boy can express his wish.

The focus in this book is on situations where a boy is often angry. There is seemingly *always* a mismatch between what he wants and the world around him, and he is difficult to live or deal with. This mismatch produces the angry outburst, the sudden physiological arousal, the ongoing propensity to anger, and at times the feeling of a family that they are 'walking on eggshells' waiting for the next confrontation. In his quieter moments a son may or may not be able to speak about the mismatch that led to his outburst. What may become clearer, if family members involved in a conflict are able to spend time talking about the outburst once things have quietened down, is that the son may not be able to explain the 'force' that seemed to come over him in the situation. The involuntary aspect of the affect of anger makes it seem to the individual that he has no choice but to respond how he did.

The main point here is that anger is a clue that there is a problem, but the emotional outbursts of anger, whilst unsettling and confronting, are not the problem itself. The solution lies beyond asking your son to control his anger. Parents have to assist their son to investigate his anger.

All the World's a Problem

During the mismatch that produces anger, a person's fundamental tendency is to see the world as a problem. Often the angered individual leaves out his own part in the creation of the problem. This presents a difficulty in dealing with people who are habitually angry. Angry people seem to have a bias towards feeling wronged and seeing other people or events in their life as 'the problem'. Anger is antithetical to being self-reflective.

The word 'externalisation' describes the process where a person habitually sees events in his or her life as the product of external causes. Simply, if something goes wrong, it is somebody else's fault. Aside from the difficulties this creates for those who have to associate with habitually angry people, the difficulty for angered individuals is that they see the solution as the world needing to change. Angered individuals commonly have little sense of their own ability to change themselves, and are more or less loudly demanding that the world needs to change. Angry boys need help to understand how they can act to change their world. This is often best achieved by showing a boy how he can act, or has acted, to change things, but which he has failed to recognise.

Chronically angry people may have what could be called the 'poor-me' view of the world. Angered people feel like victims, and often

The Nature of Anger

surround themselves with people who are ready to accommodate their whims. Angry people are good at seeing problems, but often not so great at finding solutions.

This difficulty is especially pronounced if, in addition to problems, a person has a tendency to see *positive* events as caused by external circumstances. When an angry boy is able to make it through a particularly difficult class where he has not got into trouble, or has not misbehaved at school for one month, it is rare for him to say to himself, 'I've done well in getting through this'.

This failure to see positives mean that depression and sadness, too, are common accompaniments to anger. Angry individuals are not just mad, but they are also often sad.

In angry boys the tendency to feel like a victim becomes pronounced when boys are blamed by adults (teachers and parents) for things they did not do, but which fits the boys' history of wrongdoing. Often boys who are wrongly accused end up confirming the truth of the adult's opinion of them, acting out the deed that the accusation was based on. Angry and aggressive boys generally cannot stand to take responsibility for the picture of themselves that they have created in others. The problem is seen once again as the fault of the accusing adult, and not of the expectations the young person has created. This is a problem which requires careful attention in dealing with angry young adolescents.

The Relation between Thought and Affect

A mother, Lucy, came to see me to talk about her difficulties with her son. Whilst she and her son had a long history of problems, recently he had become completely uncooperative with household chores. He did not tidy his room, take out the garbage, clean the birdcage, feed the bird, look after the dog, or mow the lawn as he had agreed to do. The situation had

The Problem

> become a struggle, with repeated loud arguments and fights. The garbage was piling up in the kitchen ('It's his job', Lucy insisted) and the bird had died because Lucy's son had not fed it. When I asked Lucy to tell me where her son's father was, she told me she had started divorce proceedings against her estranged husband some months previously.

I never had the opportunity to talk with Lucy's son—I referred him to someone else as it was clear Lucy needed to talk about her own difficulties. The point of the example above is that often in family arguments, *the participants are also arguing about something else*. I never knew the specifics of the 'something else' Lucy's son was arguing about, but it is clear the break up of a family unit may well have the effect of a son losing his wish to be part of the running of a household.

This is one of the difficulties in dealing with anger: there is often not a clear or straightforward link between the content of anger and the reasons why someone is angry. The truth of this is revealed by a situation that many parents have encountered. The parent, sick of the rages of their adolescent son, declares in the middle of an argument, 'You've been really angry since you broke up with your girlfriend'. The adolescent responds, 'No, it's you and your stupid rules that I'm angry about'.

Adolescence is centred around the fact of puberty, where the appearance of the markers of adult sexual function prompt a movement from the dependence of childhood to the independence of adulthood. Whilst there is a large variability in the age at which this occurs, the logical moment itself can be the source of conflict. The fact that the suffocating (to the adolescent) concerns of the parent are pushed aside can be an important statement of independence on the child's part. As the example of Lucy and her son shows, in matters of the adolescent's inner life the parent has been deposed from naming matters of the heart for the child. In adolescence, the parent often becomes, at best, a consultant. This needs to be taken into account in approaches to adolescents, and is covered in more detail in Chapter 4.

Anger is commonly *displaced* from one idea, situation or domain and expressed in another domain or through another idea. The fundamental displacement in anger is from an internal discontent to the angry individual finding an external problem through which to express his discontent in a rather inexact manner. Anger could be called a messy or deceiving emotion, as the reasons for the anger are often unclear. The reasons, or 'whys' of anger, can be a battleground between parents and children. This is because the affect of anger (along with many other types of affect) is opportunistic, in that anger may attach itself to an idea in order to allow itself expression. An argument about rules, tidiness or chores will be the latest in a long line of angry outbursts that give expression to quite another problem. Commonly there is not just one underlying reason for responding angrily and aggressively, but a whole series of reasons. These reasons are often specific to the individuals involved.

Battling over the 'whys' of anger tends to be fruitless. The battle usually ends up being about parent and child attempting to enforce their views of the problem on the other. Fruitlessness results as both parties attempt to impose certainty when there is clearly doubt, both for the boy about his own intentions and for the parent attempting to guess his or her child's intentions.

Simply put, when conflict occurs in a family, it is important to keep one's ears open for the 'something else' that the arguments may be about. It may prove very valuable in solving the problem.

Anger and Ambivalence

Anger is often related to other emotions, and in fact anger may be an emotion that occurs amongst an assortment of others. The much over-used jargon for this in psychology is 'ambivalence'—where an individual feels more than one emotion at one time.

That more than one emotion can be present simultaneously is an idea beyond many young adolescents. It may be safer, easier and more certain to express anger, rather than the myriad emotions and notions that surround the anger. These can include sadness, anxiety, self-doubt, uncertainty, shame … Anger is often the tip (and much of the submerged portion) of the iceberg of emotions. Feeling overwhelmed, an adolescent may feel as if disintegration would result from admitting to the hidden, dangerous emotions which are his only alternative to striking out. One of the tasks of an adult is to help an adolescent deal better with the complexities of emotional experience. Steps for increasing an adolescent's sophistication in emotional life are covered in Part II of the book.

Anger and Relationships

Anger is primarily an emotion that is based in relationships: it is most often directed by an adolescent towards those with whom he has some sort of social relationship. First and foremost, *anger is a relationship-based emotion.*

As a means of exploring the themes above—in particular, how anger appears in relationships—I will now outline some case studies that contextualise the ideas I have introduced. These cases show that it is not just any particular cause (if by 'cause' we mean an event) that brings about difficulties with anger, but also the way an individual has positioned himself in relation to others. These examples illustrate some of the mismatches between a boy and his social environment that lead to the emotion of anger. They reflect a way of thinking about conflict that may help adults understand the anger of adolescent boys. By understanding this way of thinking, rather than reacting to the problem as if it were only the angry outburst, adults may find constructive methods of responding to conflict.

The Nature of Anger

It should be remembered that these case studies are illustrative, and that aspects of each may or may not be involved in any individual case. Certainly we should be prepared to find something completely unexpected behind the symptom of anger in each young person that we deal with.

> Alan, a 13-year-old boy, is teased in the schoolyard regarding his sexual preferences. He reacts quickly and angrily, pulling a metal ruler from his bag and hacking into the necks of his classmates, wounding their necks. One of the boys Alan attacks requires admission to hospital. After Alan has a tearful, remorse-filled encounter with the deputy principal, the school's head of student welfare asks me to talk with Alan about his anger. The principal, clearly the angry one now, says, 'He's a nice boy but he just won't do what he says he will. This is his last chance. If you can't help him control his anger, and this happens again, he is going to be expelled.'

My initial meeting with Alan was similarly filled with tears, remorse and many promises to 'not be bad again'. I had been told that his remorse was a familiar script to the school authorities. He appeared to be genuinely remorseful, but from the information the school had given me, it seemed his remorse counted for little if he was provoked. Unlike the majority of his peers, even the threat of dire consequences from the principal appeared to have little effect in helping him stay inside the school rules of reasonable conduct. There appeared to be a force operating within Alan that was stronger than any of these factors.

At a second meeting Alan revealed that he could not stand that someone else thought he was 'a faggot', and that the classmates who were teasing him seemed so smug and self-satisfied that he felt he had to strike them. This seemed to be the first mismatch involved in Alan's angry outburst. His rules for maintaining his view of himself contravened the school's rules: his rules, his retaliation upon his classmates with his ruler, were different from the rules of the school.

'I am not wrong about myself': mirroring and the fear of disintegration

Peers form an important function in adolescence. For most teenagers, peer groups are the primary means of social expression. It is within the peer group that an important 'mirroring function' occurs, which assists an adolescent maintain a coherent self-image. In their social environment, adolescents encounter friends, classmates and enemies who reflect back a more or less coherent view of the adolescent as a whole, integrated person. As adolescence progresses, the importance of these peers tends to increase, and the importance of the mirroring function of the family tends to decrease, although family, particularly parental figures, maintain an importance throughout life as they are associated with the origins of the individual.

We all carry with us a more or less conscious idea of a unified image of ourselves, a sense of who we are as individuals. When this sense is attacked or threatened, by someone who seems to be far more successful or beautiful than us, or by someone who directly challenges us regarding our competence, authority and the like (including our own teenage children), it is likely to destabilise this coherent image of ourselves.

Peers come to act as a sort of mirror. We tend to think negatively about those peers who reflect a negative image of ourselves. In some cases, we can think that our own self-image is threatened with disintegration: it seems we might 'fall apart' in comparison to strong or competent others. Anger (and resulting aggression) can be seen as an assertion of our own self-image above how we think someone else is devaluing us. In short, anger is a statement: 'I am not wrong about myself'.

The Nature of Anger

Alan's aggression can be seen as a protective act, attacking the unity or wholeness of those whose taunts threaten him with disintegration. Within angry individuals, the fundamental psychic tendencies can be very different from the face that is shown to the world. Rather than the aggressive, swaggering tough guy we might expect, we find a boy who is fragile and vulnerable and reliant on the constant affirmations of those around him. However, precisely because this is how things are organised, his fragility cannot be approached directly.

This is a major problem in speaking with such boys about their difficulties with anger. How can problems about their behaviour be discussed without triggering the defensive reaction 'I am not wrong about myself'? These difficulties are compounded as it often appears to the boy that the aggressive act, such as screaming at his parents, solves the problem and is thus the best way to respond. However, the repetition of aggressive acts results in marginalisation, then suspension, and finally expulsion from school, or ongoing punishments and a negative atmosphere within the family. An 'excluded' status is often perceived by an aggressive boy as victimisation, and he considers himself a rightful avenger for what has been done to him. He may avenge himself until he has reached the margins of his family or social group, classmates, and school. Violent, vengeful acts are ultimately self-destructive. The consequences of these acts tend to have a negative effect on life opportunities for the boy. Adolescence is a time where intervention can occur before the opportunities disappear.

This fear of disintegration also gives a clue as to the arbitrariness of whether anger is directed in or out. The assertion of anger—'I am not wrong about myself'—and the attack that follows on those perceived as the source of the false assertion, is not far from the statement 'I am wrong about myself' leading to an attack on the self. Anger refutes the reflected image whereas an acceptance of the image gives rise to sadness, depression and attacks on the self. This is why boys who are aggressive may show a worrying degree of somewhat arbitrary self-destructiveness and recklessness. Anger may have an important protective function against sadness and depression. Merely making it a boy's task to reduce or manage the expression of anger may bring about increases in other negative emotions.

For Alan, his problem seemed to be that the teasing of classmates in the schoolyard easily smashed his ideas about himself. In addition, his view of himself was influenced by the wrath of his school's deputy principal. His permeability to others' views of him tosses him between anger and remorse *with little prospect of him being able to determine what he wants for himself*. Questions such as 'Who am I?' and 'What do I want?' are central but difficult questions for adolescents. They are only ever answered partially and provisionally, and can rarely be approached directly.

However, in Alan's case, his permeability to others means that he is always looking to what others want of him, rather than what he wants himself. This means the question of what he wants is not asked. Central to assisting him was the discussion of these questions. Such a discussion cannot occur in the shadow of Alan's (or any boy's) guilt and remorse, tempting though it may be. The guilt and remorse of an angry boy tend to reassure us that he has had the correct moral response to a crisis situation, but Alan's remorse was a response to what the school authorities had expressed to him in clear terms and was Alan's way of accommodating what the school wanted of him.

However, the source of Alan's anger is more worthy of investigation than condemnation. His anger brings us closer to his self-perception and its disturbance by the accusation in the schoolyard. The cry of 'That's not what I want' inherent in the angry act may be at least a start on the road of a helping a boy to answer the question of what he wants.

I'll Do What I Like

John found the school system to be oppressive. He disliked the uniform, the commands from teachers that had to be followed, the regimented timetable. He was often late for class, dragging his feet down the school's corridors where he was repeatedly found by the deputy principal, or was reprimanded by the class teacher when he eventually made it to class. John found these reprimands difficult to bear. He would fly into a rage, feeling misrepresented, and perpetrate all kinds of acts that would result in him being given lunchtime and after-school detentions, and occasionally suspensions. He felt persecuted and victimised by the school staff, whom John felt had no idea of who he really was apart from a 'troublemaker'. This was the mismatch for John: he did not feel he fitted into the school system, and that the teachers' ideas about him were not who he really was.

During a therapy group for aggressive boys at his school, in answer to a question from one of the other boys in the group, John gave the following description of an incident he had been involved in the previous month:

> ... that little bastard, we were really getting into him. He got it bad, man! There were four of us getting him. He just started crying, but we were sick of him. We had him on the ground kicking him. There was one time where I had this ring [shows to group] and I had his head and I hit him with my fist and it left this mark on his cheek. [group laughs] It was so good ... he had to go to hospital ...

When I asked John what had provoked the attack he gave a number of answers, all of which seemed trivial (e.g., the victim's pants were too short) and which provoked laughter

The Problem

> from the group. Further, it seemed that whilst there was some generalised anger and discontent directed at the victim, he had done little to provoke the attack, which was planned the day before amongst John and his friends.

Whatever exaggerations are involved in the retelling of the story, this illustrates a further function of anger and aggression: to promote a certain image of a boy's own self to his peers. The image that John was trying to create is one of a man who could do whatever he liked. He seemed to be immune to the consequences of his actions with teachers, police, parents, the injuries to the boy and the on-going problems the attack caused for the victim. In his retelling, we find in John not a fear of disintegration but an enjoyment in the telling, as it shored up John's sense of himself as an aggressive, tough, all-conquering individual. In the fantasy that he built about the attack, John painted himself as someone relatively free of the restrictions that he had to suffer in his day-to-day life at school. His friends listened admiringly to his account, which hid the unsure and troubled aspects of his encounters with teachers and other authority figures.

In talking about the event, John's fundamental assertion seems to be (in a variation on Alan's fundamental assertion) 'I am right about myself'. Despite all of the difficulties of his life, he is still someone who can do what he likes. The fact that aggression is necessary to assert that he is right about himself makes it clear that there is a degree of doubt about whether John is in fact right about himself. And whilst doubt about ourselves is something we all share, John's use of aggression to assuage this doubt caused many problems for him.

John clearly enjoyed retelling the story; his need to enjoy himself as the transgressor of limits others have to obey reveals an absence of enjoyment in other areas of his life. Why should he accept limits when this is his only means of enjoyment?

The problem for John was that this attempt to shore himself up had very real consequences. For example, he was suspended from school following the incident he described. The police were called, although he was not charged. John also managed to pick up a reputation at the school that meant he was the first one blamed for acts of misbehaviour and violence there. Eventually he was forced to leave the school and attend another. However, John's story had a better ending than these events suggest. I will return to his story, and the problem of limits and enjoyment, at the start of Part II.

If fear of disintegration is one factor in the problem of aggression, enjoyment of the position an aggressive status affords a boy in his peer group is another (see Chapter 4 for further discussion of this problem). Whilst the process of using his peers to reflect a sense of himself is at play, in the same way as it was in the case of Alan, in this instance John is clearly enjoying himself as he tells his story.

The Persecuted Victim

At the same time as playing the 'tough guy', John also felt very persecuted within school. He told me that he was sick of being angry and sick of being blamed for things he had not done by his teachers. He was repeatedly in conflict with teachers after they accused him. For John, this blame took on a persecutory flavour: it was as if he had turned his own sense of right and wrong on to his teachers and felt persecuted by this sense from without. He told me that the teachers in the school were always ready to tell him off and correct him. They had the wrong view of him.

This persecuted feeling results from another mismatch—similar to Alan's—'I am not who you say I am'. John felt this incorrect view of him was asserted every time that he encountered a teacher, which meant he reacted all the more strongly to the accusation. Every attempt to correct him by a school representative, no matter how simple or small—on his uniform, on fitting in with the school timetable, where his textbooks were—he heard as if he was being accused by some ugly, persecutory ogre.

The extraordinary point here is that whilst John had clearly been a persecutor in the attack he described to the group, he also thought of himself as the persecuted one. This is a feature of the 'one-way' ethics that angry and aggressive boys seem to have: they are often blind to the problems of others, yet hypersensitive to slight criticisms directed at themselves.

Perhaps most importantly, this position of being persecuted created a crisis for John. He realised that the reputation he had created for himself at school had real effects, and he was not easily able to 'get rid' of his reputation. The crisis was that he realised he would not be able to advance in school as far as he might have liked, as he had been threatened with suspension and expulsion on several occasions. If he was to do something about this, he had to change his view of himself as the persecuted one. This switch in world view on the part of the boy is discussed further in Chapter 8, where I outline a method for changing reputations.

Raising Problems with Angry Adolescents

In raising a problem with an angry adolescent, it is best to do so with the adolescent's viewpoint and interests in mind. Don't forget that the fundamental problem in anger is that the young person sees the problems as everyone else's, not his own. Attempts to locate the young person as the source of the problem will most likely only exacerbate the difficulties, or at least have adolescents make agreements they cannot keep (as in the case of Alan).

If an adolescent's viewpoint is not clear, this needs to be clarified with the young person. Steps for doing this are outlined in detail in Chapter 5, but there are a few important brief points for now.

- Most young people find anger unpleasant. Alan and John both complained to me that they disliked feeling angry and wished to do something about the situations that led to their anger. The aversive nature of anger means it is *in the adolescent's interest to do something about it*. As a general principle, don't expect an adolescent to do something unless there is something in it for him, particularly if he regularly feels aggrieved by others in his family, school or social group.

- If it is difficult to find anything in behaviour or attitude that is in the adolescent's interest to change, at least raise the problem as one that acknowledges the social context. Try to find out what wrong (presumably perpetrated by another) the adolescent's anger was a response to, however unreasonable it might seem. *Acknowledge that it was a response* before going on to discuss the problematic aspects of the boy's response. Productive discussions are not likely to occur without this acknowledgement.

- Several factors will prevent an adult from successfully discussing the anger or aggression with an adolescent. First, if the adult is angry, then he or she is unlikely to be able to easily identify something that is in the adolescent's interest, or acknowledge that the adolescent was responding to some wrong. *Wait until you have calmed down*. Second, if you are not 'in touch' with an adolescent, and thus know his comings and goings and his likes and dislikes, the process of finding out what is in his interests and acknowledging what he is responding to is going to be significantly more difficult. *A strong relationship both builds goodwill to discuss difficult issues and gives the adult a head start in knowing the adolescent's likely responses*.

In Brief

- The actual expression of anger is not usually the problem, but a clue to the problem. Anger is contagious and parents should resist this contagion.

- Anger is a perception of 'a wrong' outside the angry individual, which the angry individual perceives as unfair. Anger is an expression of discontent cast onto others. This makes sorting out problems with angry people difficult, as angry adolescents tend to see the problem, and the solution, as external to themselves.
- Anger is, first and foremost, a relationship-based emotion. It is within the context of how a boy views and negotiates his relationships that his tendency to anger can be best understood.
- The emotion of anger is opportunistic. As well as being easily displaced from inside to outside, it is also easily displaced from one situation to another. The solution to anger may not even be to do with what the young person is angry about.
- Anger can be seen as an assertion: 'I am not wrong about myself'. This assertion is often against a 'psychical danger' from the outside that threatens the individual in some manner.
- Anger may be one amongst a range of emotions and ideas expressed in response to a difficulty an adolescent is experiencing.
- Anger and accompanying aggression can also be an enjoyment, or assertion of an elevated status.
- Anger is a problem when the response and the provocation seem out of proportion to each other. Reports from school are usually a reliable indicator that there is a problem.
- Effectively raising problems with angry adolescents can really only be done if the adult is not angry and is 'in touch' with the young person.
- Problems are most easily solved when they are raised in a way that does not locate the young person as the sole problem, but acknowledge that the young person's actions were a response to a situation.

2
Aggression, Anger and Ethics

Aim at what is intermediate in passions and in actions ... any one can get angry—that is easy— ... but to do this to the right person, to the right extent, at the right time, with the right aim, and in the right way, that is not for everyone, nor is it easy; that is what goodness is, rare and noble.

Aristotle, *Nicomachean Ethics*

The cases of Alan and John, discussed in the previous chapter, clarify that anger is an emotion that emerges when the stability of one's self-image is threatened from without. Aggression, the act of physically damaging or destroying something or someone in the world, emerges when this threat becomes unbearable. The angered individual can no longer stand the tension created by the threat to his status and strikes as a way to maintain his self-image. In this way *aggression can be seen as an act which aims at 'psychical homeostasis'*; that is, the aggressor is simply attempting to maintain a stable and coherent image of himself.

Aggression is a physical act responding to the physical arousal inside the aggressor's body. What eludes the aggressor is speech. In bypassing speech, the aggressive act bypasses the codes—reasoning, doubt, ability to wonder—that are contained in the act of speaking.

Alan's aggression was a response that brought instant results, stopping the provocation and (presumably) relieving his bodily tension. Retorting with insults, going to the deputy principal to complain, organising a program of subtle retribution by exclusion amongst his friends, are all responses less perfect, more open to doubt and less complete than the response of physical aggression.

At a fundamental level, the task with aggressive boys is to assist them *to use words rather than fists*. It requires a degree of containment (speaking takes time and the results are often not immediately apparent or able to be perceived by the aggressor) and ability to withstand frustration (the results of speech are less exact, more imperfect than aggression). Practical advice on helping aggressive boys to use speech is covered in Part II.

Sub-types of Aggression

Within the concept of aggression there are several sub-types of aggression; this discussion does not attempt to cover them all, but two sub-types are implied by the cases in Chapter 1. Alan's response can be seen as a case of *reactive aggression*—an openly confrontational expression of physical aggression in response to provocation or the frustration of a goal. It is to be contrasted with the *instrumental aggression* (also known as proactive and predatory aggression) that John showed. Instrumental aggression is aggression directed at obtaining some sort of goal. Instrumental aggression is often more planned in nature than reactive aggression, more covert and less openly confrontational—although this was not the case in the mob aggression used by John and his allies. There is an important difference between these two types of aggression.

Reactively aggressive boys respond to a situation of perceived unjustness—the 'it's not fair' of anger—but seem unable to judge what is in their best interests in a situation where they have been provoked. They are therefore unable to judge when they have gone too far, as in the case of Alan. However, as with Alan, reactively aggressive boys are able to be rational and sensible in quieter moments. Aggression comes about when they are somehow possessed by the 'temporary madness' of anger and act in a manner contrary to all they have agreed to. It should not be forgotten that what possesses the angry boy may be other reasons than the one that is presented at the time.

This contrasts with instrumentally aggressive boys, who use aggression calculatedly towards some goal. Such boys tend to be more socially skilled, competent and more liked by their peers than reactively aggressive boys. This 'cool' type of aggression appears to assist many boys without doing too much damage to their situation. Indeed, it appears that most teenage boys survive in the schoolyard by using some form of instrumental aggressiveness. Boys tend to threaten or imply aggressiveness (that is, not a physical act) and more rarely utilise actual aggression (a physical act).

Three central factors seem to separate reactively aggressive boys from their more socially successful and instrumentally aggressive counterparts. First, instrumentally aggressive boys appear to be able to use the threat of consequences calculatedly towards some goal. This strongly implies that these boys have a *capacity for thought and reflection* that exceeds their reactively aggressive counterparts. Second, socially capable and instrumentally aggressive boys are able to reflect more carefully on their relationships and have the *capacity to understand the world from another's point of view*. Socially successful boys have a sense of the importance of their relationships and what advantages are given by or can be gained from these relationships. Finally, socially skilled boys have a *belief in their capacity to act* to change the environment. They believe that what they do and say makes a difference. These three dimensions are often absent or diminished in reactively angry boys. These three capacities, once developed, can be viewed as 'antidotes' to anger and physical aggression and this is discussed more fully in Chapter 5.

The major point here is that an aim of ending all anger and aggression is unrealistic and possibly counter-productive. Utilising the rush of anger and the impulse to aggression in a more refined, socially constructive manner may bear more fruit.

Another aspect of instrumental aggression is the enjoyment of the image that the aggression promotes of the aggressor amongst his peers: the aim of the aggressor is to perpetrate aggression for his own enjoyment. This type of aggressiveness has its extreme expression in the sadistic psychopath, depicted crudely in many Hollywood films. The psychopath derives pleasure simply from the act itself, which he plays out in front of an imagined audience. Here, the remorse or guilt that is commonly felt after acts of aggression (as with Alan) is overshadowed or blocked by the pleasure of the act. Such extremes are met somewhat rarely, and we are concerned here with the more common forms of reactive and instrumental aggression.

Acts of aggression cannot always be defined as reactive or instrumental. Aspects of each type may be present in any individual and any aggressive act.

In summary, aggressive acts may be more or less a mixture of anger, enjoyment and self-preservation. Not all aggression is angry aggression. There is also some logical justification for arguing that during and after adolescence there is a developmental move in some cases from reactive to instrumental aggression. As the reactively aggressive boy negotiates the tumult that results from his openly aggressive style, he may alter his stance to a more planned and covertly aggressive one. This will be the case particularly if he cultivates beliefs in the context of his social group that justify the expression of aggression.

Anger, Aggression and Ethics

The idea of 'psychical homeostasis' provides an explanation of aggression. However, such explanations are a long way from the experience of the person against whom the aggression is directed. The urge to action involved in anger nearly always spills over into some sort of communicative behaviour. Aside from outright physical aggression, the expression of the emotion of anger can also be intimidating. Glaring, long tension-filled silences, tensed muscles, loud voices, yelling and physical violence belong on a continuum that implies an intention to act. Anger, the emotion, and aggression, the act, are not altogether separable.

The glaring, posture and loudness of voice may be perceived as a form of psychological aggression and is commonly regarded as such. The time interval between the object of the anger fearing he or she may be attacked and an angered individual forming the conscious intent to harm is variable. What is taken to be aggressive is subjective, with the difference between anger and aggression being not altogether clear.

This lack of a clear separation between anger and aggression often means that those around an angry person experience his demeanour and attitude as aggressive, and feel his expression of anger—which is taken to be aggression—to be unjustified and 'wrong'. This may be despite the angry adolescent having no intention of actually causing physical harm or damage. In turn, it means the angry adolescent himself feels wronged by such an accusation from others. It is easy to see how such situations, in the hot-house of family relations or in the pressure of the classroom, can escalate out of control.

What the angry and aggressive person is focused on is his internal state and attempting to remove the anxiety or the anger-provoking stimulus that is causing this state. He is trying to correct the fact that he 'feels wronged'. It is also how the one whom the angry person is threatening feels: wronged by the other's anger.

This leads to two very differing accounts of the same situation, one from the angry person and the other from the one with whom he is angry. These differing accounts of the situation are the cause of ongoing and escalating conflict in which the two combatants feel they have no way to escape. Like gladiators in the Colosseum, the conflict becomes a 'fight to the death' and much lasting damage to the relationship of parent and child, or teacher and student, can be caused by such events.

Now whilst the two people have differing accounts of the conflict, structurally they are trying to do the same thing: prove each other wrong. This leads to the contagion of anger. One angry person in the household can make everyone else angry—'bringing them down to his level'—as he faces off with various members of the family.

Anger and aggression involve a focus on the wrong-doing of another. The joint accusers enter an escalating cycle where the means of solving the problem is very quickly lost. Rather, the angered ones become consumed by a moral dance. For each partner, his or her adversary slips into being the evil one. There is a certain amount of symmetry and mirroring in this relationship. Although opposed in content (whatever the content might be: bedtime, homework, Xbox), the pair are doing the same thing: trying to prove each other 'wrong'. The real evil is the moral dimension itself, for it only serves to distract both parties from the ends they are trying to achieve.

The Hebrew word 'Satan' simply means 'adversary'. In modern usage, Satan has come to represent evil and wrong-doing that was not apparent in the Old Testament. This slippage of the meaning of the devil's name from foe to the Lord of Evil points to a tendency we all share: to confuse those who stand in our way with evil-doers. This tendency is pronounced in anger, where a problem with means (pursuing one's own ends) collapses into a moral judgement. If someone gets in our way we don't tend to see a practical problem that needs to be solved, but we cry: 'That's wrong!', 'He can't do that!', or 'It's not fair!'. We tend to think of adversaries who get in our way as more than just opponents: adversaries are also evil, and morally inferior. Over time, the 'evilness' takes over and the problem with objectives is forgotten, taking second place. This collapsing of means into morals is contagious: angry people produce anger in others.

The contagiousness of anger means it does not occur to the angry combatants that their battle is possibly making the situation worse, or that their anger may be caused by the way they are viewing the situation. Anger is antithetical to self-reflection and reason. Although the dispassionate observer may easily be able to see the unfolding disaster, this is not at all apparent to the angry person.

The parental objective that the 'evil' adolescent is interfering with is most commonly the parent trying to ensure the adolescent makes it to the end of his teens relatively unscathed. The perversity of this situation is not lost on most parents, who, after an angry exchange, can easily become unsure which way to turn to recover a stance where they can speak and act with authority and offer guidance.

Ideally, in such a confrontation, the parent should either refuse to take up this angry mirroring or must act to call an end to it once they realise it has begun. The parent is the one who must take the step of reflection and self-responsibility, as these qualities are only just emerging in the adolescent. To parent an adolescent (as opposed to a child) means a parent creates some distance between him- or herself and the adolescent. It is something that the stage of adolescence calls for. Repeated argument, conflict and anger often tend to break down this distance, resulting in a hostile, close and suffocating emotional contact. Somehow parents have to find a way to step back from such a relationship, allowing, guiding an adolescent to find his own way.

At the same time, it is essential during adolescence—particularly what looks to be shaping as a troubled or stormy adolescence—that parents stay in touch and involved with their son. Abandoning their son to his rages, his seemingly inflexible, uncaring and rigid assertions that 'I'll do and say as I like', and allowing him to live in a moral and ethical desert during his adolescence, is an option that many parents cannot allow. Finding a way to assist an angry adolescent to reflect on moral and ethical difficulties is not easy.

To summarise, the problem of being wronged revolves around the difficulty of morals or ethics. Both parties in a conflict feel that they have 'right' on their side. The problem of ethics or morals is the central concern of this chapter. It is one level that parents can maintain something of a distance appropriate to adolescence and yet intervene in the difficulties their son is experiencing. This does not mean asserting that the parental guide to acting is superior to the son's. Rather, ethics is a ground upon which a parent can assist the son by enhancing the natural advancements of adolescence. The Doing Anger Differently method, explained more fully in Part II, is to explore with the son the various positions he adopts, with the aim of helping him to develop his own view on the rights and wrongs, the positives and negatives of his actions and ways of relating to others in the world.

The remainder of this chapter will attempt to help adults to understand the ethics of conflict in a way that uses the difference in the accounts of the angry person and the one with whom he is angry.

Aggression and Ethics

One of the problems encountered by adults who deal with angry young people is how to persuade a boy to accept a limit on the use of physical aggression. Whether feelings of anger, enjoyment-seeking or anxiety promote an aggressive act, aggression can be seen as a problem of how a boy can accept a limit on reacting as he wants to. In times when he is not possessed by angry emotions, the boy is able to make any number of sensible agreements—which may disappear in the heat of emotional arousal.

One of the important factors here is an ethical or moral order as the boy understands it on the one hand, and the family and institutions he has to deal with on the other. Usually there appears to be a conflict between how a boy justifies his acts, as with John in

Chapter 1, and the sort of behaviour that a school can allow. Staff from many institutions who encounter acts such as John's usually see someone like him as without morals. However, a close reading of John's case shows that he is very caught up with the moral and ethical concerns of being treated fairly.

His case is not an exceptional one. Moral questions abound in boys who are angry and aggressive. Such emotions and acts are linked to the question of action to gain reparation or to right wrongs for which the world has been perceived to be responsible. Moral concerns apply both to the individual's perceptions of another's actions (the angered individual perceives that he has right on his side), to his own action (I am therefore justified in taking this action), and to others' evaluations of the angry individual's action.

So it is not correct to assert that aggressive boys are lacking in moral codes. Recognising this gives a starting point for discussion. It is important to understand the boy's moral code, what he believes to be right or wrong, and take this as a basis for development.

Enhancing Ethics

The aim of adults is to *enhance or widen the boy's already existing ethical and moral views*. Commonly, an aggressive boy acts as if there is an independent moral order which supports his view of the world. Whenever a demand is made on the boy he refers to this 'other', inner order. The fact that the world does not fit into his way of viewing things causes a great deal of tension that he cannot stand and aggression is a method of making the world fit. This 'other' order, his view of the way the world 'should' be, then justifies his aggression, regardless of the consequences.

I once saw a video installation, 'Crossing', by Korean artist June Bum Park. It was a ten-minute footage of a busy city intersection, taken from an overhead camera high above. Crowds of people poured across the intersection or stopped according to the pedestrian lights,

The Problem

and cars raced across when permitted by the traffic lights. The video was speeded up by perhaps ten times, and thus what one sees is how people as a collective obey the rules as indicated by lights. This seemingly mindless obedience to rules is illustrated many times within the film *Koyanisqaatsi*, by Godfrey Reggio and Philip Glass, via a similar technique. The artist in the case of the video installation went one step further: he had superimposed two giant hands over the footage which made it appear as if it were the hands that the pedestrians and the drivers were obeying—a pair of omnipotent hands which could not be crossed or disobeyed. Thus the paradoxical title of the piece. There was no one crossing the law of the hands in order to cross the street. The paradox is further developed by the truth that there is a freedom to be found inside the law that one keeps.

This illustrates the differences and intertwining between the child's, adult's and adolescent's moral functioning. In the child's experience a pair of hands is indeed as physical as the artist makes them appear in the video: a parent will physically bar the child's progress as he heedlessly steps from the pavement into oncoming traffic. The child has not yet internalised the pair of hands of the video, or if he has, it is because the parent insists that the child wait to cross the road while the pedestrian light is red. There is no other reason to stop at the kerb than the rule explained by the parent. Conversely, each adult in the artist's video has his own way of being submissive to the rule, which is partly in his or her interest and in the interest of the smooth functioning of a society. This gives the hands a god-like character.

For the adult, this seemingly uniform, seemingly mindless obedience to the rules at the traffic and pedestrian lights hides many reasons for keeping the rules. An adult may have too much to risk losing—a family, a new car, a job that is enjoyed, a promising future—or actually enjoy being part of the order that the rules create, or simply be in a reflective mood where time is not a pressure ... the list is endless. My point is that each adult has his or her own mix of reasons for keeping to rules at a particular time.

This seems to show that there are in fact two laws. One is written in the statutes of the state or country, which enables the policeman to fine a citizen for jaywalking or running a red light. There is a second law, beyond this written law, which is manifested in a different way in each individual. The giant hands of the video seem to show that everyone mindlessly obeys the same law. However, this obscures the fact that each person will have his or her own reasons for obeying the law as well as personal difficulty in doing so. It is this process of an individual finding his or her own law, a law beyond the law of the land, to which we must pay attention in the case of the angry and aggressive adolescent.

The adolescent impatiently looks at the traffic, trying to find a break in the line of cars in order to skip across the road quickly, feeling that the rule of waiting until the lights are green doesn't apply to him. The hands become provisional, permeable, subject to the adolescent's desires. And where is the parent? The parent steps back from the kerb the adolescent departs from, is at the other kerb as the adolescent arrives, even talks to the adolescent as he crosses, saying in the adolescent's ear: Why this risk? Why is this haste so important? This is where you have told me you are going. Is it worth risking being knocked down here?

In adolescence, it is a matter of crossing, experimenting, pushing, in order to find a law, the law that each individual discovers. Adolescence demonstrates that each individual has to find his own way to his own version of the law, which involves ignoring, or contravening, or dispensing in some way the law that is laid down in writing. What I am arguing here is that there is a law beyond the legal law of the land, beyond any rules of a group or a school, a law beyond that law indicated by the hands in the video. It is this internal law that each individual must find for himself and take up, whether he knows it or not.

The difference between these two laws—the law of the land as against the internal law, how what is right or wrong is manifested in each individual—is important to keep in mind. This is because the keeping of written law is particularly problematic in the case of an angry adolescent. As I pointed out in Chapter 1, anger is the result of a mismatch between the angered individual's own law and the expectations of others—society's laws, school laws and family rules. The aggressive adolescent's attempt to take the law into his own hands causes quite a problem. An adult has to assist an angry adolescent in the process of finding his own way to keeping the written law.

Pro-social, Anti-social

In Alan's moment of anger, his rules of vengeance overshadowed any codes that he was bound by in the school or a wider social context—he had to destroy his classmates. John's manner of retelling his story was aimed at showing that he did not have to fit into the rules like other people. In each case, the boy follows his rules and ideas of how the world should be, so that he seems unable to understand that other people might work with different rules. Aggressive adolescents often do not even attempt to understand, or they simply ignore how their actions impact on others. For example, in the case of John, after he told his story to the group I asked him to explain in more detail precisely what the victim's injuries were that required going to hospital. I also asked him about the look on his victim's face after he punched him in the head. John became uneasy with this conversation and tried to immediately change the subject. He simply was not prepared to think about this aspect of his actions. Eventually, his story is a success, precisely because he was able to find a way to keeping the rules and thus, paradoxically, found a freedom to act as he wished.

How can difficult topics be approached, when boys try to shut down any conversation that puts them in a less-than-flattering light? This problem has been targeted within many programs aimed at aggression and anger reduction.

Recent approaches in the field tend to aim at establishing 'pro-social behaviour' (where an individual acts in a manner that takes into account others' needs and wishes) and discouraging 'anti-social behaviour' (behaviour that ignores or denies others' needs and wishes). The basic idea is that angry and aggressive boys are too 'ego-centric' and need to become more 'socio-centric'.

Such an analysis has some truth in it. I have conducted many therapy groups in mainstream schools for angry and aggressive boys. When boys first come to these groups, they arrive as if they are saying, 'I am going to act exactly in accordance with how I feel'. When someone in the group provokes them and they become angry, the boys respond with aggression. This meets the boys' short-term aim of reducing tension and maintaining 'psychical homeostasis'.

How does one induce a boy to become more 'socio-centric'? Attempts have been made to teach boys moral reasoning. If adolescents can reason more effectively, so the psychologist argues, and learn higher forms of ethical thinking above the simple 'if he hurts me then I hurt him', then he will be able to 'see the bigger picture' and not act so aggressively. Unfortunately, such approaches have had limited success, mainly because rational approaches fall away in the heat of the moment. No amount of reasoning will help Alan feel less persecuted by his classmates in the example in Chapter 1.

Other approaches—such as those by authors Robert Bly and Steve Biddulph—have suggested we should teach boys to become 'true men', which they have ceased being able to do because of constraints of the modern Western world. The argument of such books is that boys need to learn to become real men, and the definition of a man is tied to the natural world and includes (among other things) a respect for other people; in addition, there is a natural masculinity that boys should aspire to, and this natural masculinity involves a respect for the law.

These claims are in the same category as the aggressive boy's claim that there is a moral order that exists 'out there' to support a certain mode of acting. But appealing to a natural masculinity is instituting one moral order over another. It tends to ignore the fundamental problem: boys break the social rules with their aggression because they cannot bear or cope with what they feel at the moment of persecution.

The Ethics of Self-interest

I have found in my work with aggressive boys in therapy groups that, over time, the group members respond to a boy who deals with provocation via aggression by distancing themselves—and perhaps even feeling they cannot be in the same group as the very aggressive boy. When a boy in the group continues to act in this way, by hitting someone each time there is a difficulty or a problem, most boys will not wish to come back. There will be no group for the boys to continue attending.

Now, if the group has met for long enough so that the members have come to value the group and enjoy it, this creates a dilemma for them. To continue to act aggressively in the group will destroy a place they like to be in at school. Putting this problem to the group has boys thinking about the manner in which they will have to act to preserve the group. This is simply a question of *boys acting in their own self-interest to preserve something they want*. Once this question is discussed in the group, boys then have a reason to act in a manner that means they tolerate some of the tension of their negative emotions. Boys will only act in accordance with some socially agreed norms if they *feel they have something to lose by crossing these norms*.

So in order to preserve the group, boys do not try to gratify themselves immediately by hitting someone and providing the release of tension that this brings. Rather, they act in accordance with ethics or morals that preserve the group. *Each boy must find his own way to act in a manner that will preserve the group.* This contrasts sharply with others (parents, teachers, other adults) telling or teaching them how to act. If there is one key point to be made about assisting adolescent boys to 'set their own limits' it is this: *adolescent boys have to find their own ways of keeping the rules.* This can really only be done once boys discover 'what is in it' for them. I call this the creation of a 'crisis of possibility', where a boy begins to understand that his aggression is ultimately self-destructive.

However, boys do not have to be in a therapy group in order for these problems to be raised. Techniques to promote this kind of thought and discussion in adolescents are covered in Chapters 6 and 7. For now, the secret of working with adolescents is not to tell, but to discuss, show, question and perhaps guide them to their own solutions. Solutions to what? Towards finding a means of getting what they want, inside the social rules.

Self-interest and Self-destructiveness

It could be asserted that the problem with angry boys is in fact the opposite of being 'anti-social'. Rather, it could be said that aggressive boys are too 'other-focused'—in that they are continually looking to others or hitting others in order to validate their own unstable image of themselves. The approach that is required is one which focuses the boy on his individual needs and wishes, rather than always looking to the others—peers, parents, teachers and authority figures—that populate his world.

It is the manner of the way a boy reflects about his relationships that is important here. An angry and aggressive boy tends to see how his relationships diminish and destroy him, rather than how his relationships might be useful and helpful to him.

In this context remember the problem Alan had in being so permeable to others' view of him: he had never confronted the question 'What do I want?' It is only in the face of this question that Alan might have a justification for acting more 'pro-socially' amongst his peers. If a boy has little idea of what he wants, then he quite simply has nothing to lose. Why should a boy refrain from aggression when it appears to obtain for him most of the things he wants in the short term? Discussion can usefully focus on this point, what a boy can gain or lose from a future that he is creating or destroying for himself.

> A mother, Anne, came to see me about problems she was having with her son David. Anne and her husband had separated a year previously. Since well before the separation David had not liked going to school, and seldom did his housework chores. Anne and David would constantly fight about the housework, and David's father would ensure David went to school despite his reluctance. Since the separation, David became a sporadic attendee at school. He often would not get up in time, or would come home early. After a few meetings, Anne told me that her son had asked her the night before about his future. 'What do you think I should be, Mum?' Anne had responded: 'Oh, I don't mind what you do, as long as you're happy.' David's father, on the other hand, had told him that he was going to university and that was that.
>
> It seemed that both David's parents were missing the point in regard to their son. The father seemed bent on asserting his plans for David without consulting him. It was clear that David was not a high achiever at school, and it was questionable whether his father's vision was based on aptitude

> or the slightest aspiration of his son. However, Anne, without realising it, had avoided helping her son find any direction to his life. David's request was clearly for guidance, and Anne seemed unable to give any. When we discussed this point, she stubbornly stuck to her position: 'What's wrong with just wanting your boy to be happy?' After some time, she came to see that such a response gave her son no way of structuring his life towards a future goal. No wonder David did not see any point in going to school. Without an aspiration there was no point.

The vision of a future has a stabilising influence on a boy's view of himself. If a boy has a sense of some future, this makes him less vulnerable to others' whimsical views of him. He also becomes more prone to thinking about those he knows as allies rather than enemies. This instability is, of course, one of the problems of adolescence. It is a time of uncertainty and exploration that often leads to some storminess of emotions.

In summary, respect for the law, for the 'right way to act', is dependent on a boy having something to lose by transgressing the law. Something a parent (and a father in particular) can do in this regard is to show a boy how he can have what he wants, but in order to do so he must respect the law. How to transmit such a message—'You can do anything you wish, inside the law'—is a subject taken up in Chapter 3.

The Certainty of Anger and Aggression

Earlier I discussed a boy's doubts about his self-image that led to the aggressive act, and that aggression is a method of his maintaining a kind of psychical homeostasis. One function of an aggressive act is to put an end to doubt by attempting to eliminate or subjugate the source of it. However, there may be other doubts lurking in a boy's mind regarding the legitimacy of the attack. One of the functions of anger, as discussed in Chapter 1, is to ensure that *external actors* are blamed for the wrongs that the individual is reacting to. This removes a further source of doubt as to the ethics of aggression. The boy feels the individual he struck deserved it or 'had it coming to him'. The consequences of justifying the aggressive attack close down the doubts about the boy's own actions, about the ethics behind the attack and even about the doubt in the situation. It is monotonously common that the thinking and beliefs that surround the boy's post-hoc analysis of the situation are simply to justify the attack: as was the case with John's justification of his attack. Freud's insight that conscious thought is little more than justification applies here.

At times it can seem impossible to intervene to change a boy's mind during or following his anger or aggressive acting out. He seems determined to view himself as the victim of the attack and that his method of action was justified. Though this matter is dealt with more fully in Chapter 4 (see page 104), one simple point can be made here: condemning a boy's acts (although this may be important in certain cases) may leave him little room to think about the problematic aspects of his actions. If he feels condemned on a certain point, he is unlikely to consider the views of the person who is condemning him. If a boy already has a bias to blame the world for his actions, condemnation is unlikely to bring favourable results. It is more likely to deepen the problem, as the boy sees those who condemn him as having the problem. The only thing that can be done here is to create doubt—raise questions that allow the boy to experience some uncertainty about how he has acted and his justifications for it.

Morals and the Social Group

In early adolescence, there are three primary social domains: the family, the adolescent peer group and educational institutions. As adolescence proceeds, the influence of the family tends to wane and the influence of the peer group increases. It is within the peer group that an adolescent will gradually begin to practise and transform the mode of expression of his inner life that has emerged from his family. Adolescent peer groups come to be the primary mode of social expression.

Peer groups, like any other social group, develop standards of behaviour which members of the group are expected to live up to. What is exceptional about adolescent peer groups is that they represent, psychically, the first step outside the dominant influence of the family domain. Although primary school is of course important, through these years there is little influence from peers: the family remains the predominant guide. Peers are rarely influential before Grade 6, but are the dominant influence for boys by Year 8.

For youths who have a tendency to anger and aggression, this first step of extra-familial influence is doubly important. As discussed, the phenomenon of anger involves reference to an individual's particular view of a shared ethical or moral order. If angry adolescents form friendships with like-minded adolescents, who also have a view of the world that justifies their angry and aggressive 'other blaming', it can be expected to exacerbate the problem of aggression rather than place a limit on it. The problem of anti-social groupings, where adolescents form groups with similarly minded aggressors that support their aggressive actions, has been well documented.

Such a social group reflects back to the adolescent a view of himself which is congruent with his own picture of how he should be. The group may be responsible, for example, for affirming a boy's justification for aggression, or his masculine toughness (see the example of John). Such anti-social groups are a place where an aggressive 'outside the law' status is confirmed and boys feel good about not fitting in with social norms.

In addition, many boys may have difficulties changing their group identification and their view of themselves once they have been rejected by their wider peer group and have fallen in with such deviant social peers in early adolescence. At this time peers and many teachers react to a child's reputation—what they have seen and heard about him in the past—rather than his current behaviour.

With such difficulties lying in the path of an adolescent's first psychical step to independence, many parents may react by forbidding their child from associating with youngsters whose behaviour appears suspect or worrying. It may be an approach that is called for; however, it runs against the inclination towards mastery in adolescence. It may create many more fights and difficulties between the adolescent and his caregivers. That in the long run it will be 'worth it' may be correct in some cases, but not all—individual and familial factors play a strong role here.

Taking the stance of forbidding may also turn such activities of a boy 'underground'. He may associate with others and engage in activities parents do not wish him to, but they may not know about it. Forbidding undesirable contacts cuts off the adult's ability to discuss such problems openly. Rather than forbidding, it is important to be involved in discussions with the adolescent about these difficulties. If the adolescent starts to hide such things, this becomes impossible.

Aggression and 'Conscience'

I once worked with a boy who seemed to be drawn relentlessly to a game of high jinks with his teachers—indeed, with anyone in a position of authority over him.

> Fourteen-year-old Matthew seemed to love drawing his teachers into a battle. He made silly noises in class, exposed himself, destroyed school property, bullied other boys and smoked. He seemed to do these things mostly in the view of teachers. It was as if he was taunting them, daring them to mete out punishment to him. He appeared to enjoy the fact that he was breaking the

Aggression, Anger and Ethics

> rules. However, he would react with rage when teachers did intervene, often escalating the behaviour. After a few meetings in a therapy group I was conducting at his school, I noticed that Matthew had scars on his arms. I asked him about these in a private interview and he told me that at times he cut himself, often after these incidents that he provoked with teachers.

Many of the teachers at Matthew's school felt that he had no conscience, no way of setting limits for himself. He acted as if he had no understanding of the rules and how to follow them. However, through talking with Matthew in the group, it was clear he had a good understanding of what the rules were, but he enjoyed flouting them. However, it seemed that he also flouted himself.

For Matthew, it was as if he needed to have the teachers enforce the rules. The fact that he felt persecuted by teachers was merely a reflection of how he felt persecuted by his conscience. His misbehaviour was simply a manner of externalising the persecution, which perhaps provided some relief from his internal persecutions. If teachers persecuted him in response to his provocations, he did not have to persecute himself. This act, of turning external figures into a type of conscience, is a feature of both John and Alan's cases. The darker aspect of Matthew's case is that he also hurt himself. The self-harm was another means of him persecuting himself—directing his aggression towards himself. Whether the teachers were involved or he simply harmed himself seemed often to be somewhat arbitrary. I cannot write about the personal history that lies behind Matthew's difficulties, as sadly he was expelled from school during the therapy group and he refused further contact with me.

We can say generally that one of the residues that the father leaves the infant, and that stays with the son as he grows into a man, is popularly known as conscience. This formation of a 'conscience' leads to a discussion about aggression and self-destructiveness.

Recall how easily John began to feel persecuted from without. Due to the permeability of a boy's image of himself, there is often a degree of arbitrariness as to whether his aggression is directed in or out. In this sense, the provoker and the provoked are interchangeable. If an attack raises the spectre of a boy's own self-value, that his self-esteem may in fact be low, then should the provocateur be attacked for raising the spectre, or should the boy punish himself for being so worthless? In Matthew's case, he seemed to be quite aware that his ongoing provocation of the teachers was ultimately self-destructive.

The implications are that we should be careful if it seems to us that a boy has no understanding of the rules, no conscience. It may simply be that a boy's conscience is too strict.

Ethics and Rules in Adolescence

I have written about the adolescent 'inclination towards mastery'. This implies that despite lack of experience, but because of their increased cognitive capacity, adolescents would prefer to do things themselves rather than be told what to do. The full implications of this are discussed in Chapter 4 but here I will discuss the relation of these adolescent advances to the problems of ethics and anger.

Due to development of reasoning ability, adolescents are able to imagine all sorts of possibilities, some of which they may actively pursue against the advice of their elders. There is a difficult continuum between guiding and telling adolescents—letting a young person find out for himself and trying to ensure he doesn't make mistakes that have negative implications for his future. Parents, teachers and youth workers all need to be aware of what I call the 'politics of rules' with adolescents, which is a delicate mix of power, strategy, playing and skirmishes, while the adult keeps in mind the long-term best interests of the adolescent.

The problems of the 'inclination towards mastery' are exacerbated in adolescents who are angry and aggressive. Adults know that a boy acting aggressively will quickly lose many friends and educational opportunities. However, angry people don't like to be told what to do. They don't tend to believe that the problem is theirs. How can a balance be found?

The short answer is that adults need to guide adolescents to a conclusion. There is little point in trying to impose the law on rebellious adolescents. In many cases it will act as an invitation to flout the rules. In the end, no one can make an adolescent do anything. He has reached the age where he has his own mind, and agreement with rules requires his cooperation. Indeed, trying to impose rules from a position of power is often counterproductive if children are to find their own ways of 'keeping the rules'.

Unilaterally imposing rules on an adolescent generally engenders resentment in the boy, leaving him focused on how 'unfair it is', and this rearticulates his original problem. The parent as the lawmaker, imposing the rules, is seen as the problem—it is a fundamental tendency amongst angry boys. The resulting 'victim stance' leaves a boy no room to think about the problem and what he himself wants: it has been excluded by the imposition of authority. Recall in Chapter 1 that this was also a problem of anger: *in focusing on the demands of others, boys leave themselves out*. The intervention by an adult should aim to help the boy to count himself in, both as part of the problem and as the means to solve the problem.

The role of the adult is to help the adolescent *find his own subjective ways of keeping the rules*. Rather than imposing authority on an adolescent, assisting him to think about the manner in which he wants to act will ultimately pay dividends for him in developing superior moral reasoning. This means the adult should keep an open ear and mind to the ideas adolescents may take up with their peers, and discuss these ideas with him. Stopping discussions by imposing authority gives an adolescent no chance to 'try out' and experiment with ideas with parents and other caregivers, people who generally have his interests at heart.

This is a summary of the way in which adults can help boys with the reordering and 'second writing' that is adolescence. An adolescent must do the ordering and writing himself, but adults are an important guide in this. The manner in which peers can be important guides is discussed in Chapter 4.

Adolescence and 'Doing–Being'

One of the central methods adolescents, particularly male adolescents, have of gaining knowledge is through 'doing–being'. The concept of adolescence as a time of 'doing–being' has some relevance to the problem of aggression and the development of ethical thought.

Adolescents tend to want to do things first and then only later reflect on the experience. They use their own acts in the world (doing) as material to reflect on and discover who they are (being). It is often not until after an experience that adolescents have the capacity to reflect on what has happened. It is crucial to understand this in dealing with them. It is only as events unfold, discussions occur and ideas develop that the matter can perhaps be raised in detail. The knowledge cannot be 'handed down from high'. Doing followed by thinking it through is the adolescent method of gaining knowledge, usually enacted within his social group, which is his primary means of social expression.

The adults who work best with adolescents are those who understand this doing–being aspect of adolescence. Such adults use an action–reflection cycle—action followed by thinking about the action—in their discussions with young people. I developed a simple method of working with this action–reflection cycle in my work when I required a simple model of intervening into what was often the chaos of a group therapy session with eight early-adolescent males.

Simply, my model outlines key moments of intervention into the way an adolescent thinks about himself and his acts: Action—the way he sees what has happened; Description—putting words to what has happened; Meaning—the manner in which he makes meaning of what has happened. These are followed by Performing Meaning—the way he uses his understanding of the situation to act. Often, at each of the stages, angry adolescents tend to leave themselves out. We commonly find that the boy's description of the action relates what others did to him; the meaning he places on the action is often about how terrible these other people are; and the performing meaning he describes (perhaps the one place where he enters) is of how he is going to take (or has taken) revenge upon the people in his world.

The task of the adult is, by questioning and wondering at each of these four levels, to *assist the adolescent to place himself in the picture*. Sometimes it is enough to assist an adolescent to more fully describe the situation that he is talking about to allow this to happen. At other times it may be important to explore the meanings he has made of the event. In terms of the problem of aggression, the subject of this chapter, there are several approaches. Generally, after a detailed description, questions which focus on the moral framework behind the act, the 'right way to act', where limits lie, and what is unacceptable, may be the first step in explicating the boy's moral code. This moral framework may then be useful in clarifying a boy's justifications for and inconsistencies in how he acts in other areas. Simply, *the aim here is help a boy to arrive at a point where for him, he is acting ethically towards what he wants*. This theme is taken up in more detail in Part II, but for now, the simple pointers are to start with description of the action, and then later move to other meanings.

Why is this model helpful? Often, I have found that parents, teachers (from classroom assistants right up to school principals) and youth workers tend to impose their own meanings on events before understanding the young person's meaning. If you are to assist an adolescent, it is vital to understand how he views his world. Only then is it possible to help him with his difficulties. This is particularly true in the case of moral limits. If a boy gains a sense that you are judging him, or being 'moral about morals', then he is unlikely to let you know what his actual beliefs are in this regard. Problems need to be on show if they are to be worked with. However much you may disagree with a boy's standpoint, your own views should not overshadow your ability to listen to him. A helpful attitude from an adult is one of curiosity about the adolescent's viewpoint.

All this requires constant re-engagement and re-discussion of the day's or week's events with an adolescent. Perhaps one of the most important things parents can do is to keep discussing events in their son's life, no matter how trivial. Crucial here is to hold in mind the conversations with the boy—using what you have learnt about his whys and views of acting in one situation and applying them to the next. It is also possible to assist your boy with his mode of social expression amongst his peers. In addition, the parent is in the best position, having intimate daily contact with the boy, to help him verbalise his experiences of the day.

Interestingly, this is one of the most important effects of the groups that I conduct for aggressive boys. I often meet with the parents of boys in the group I have just conducted, in order to discuss what they have noticed (or not) about their sons. Commonly parents state that the main change has been in their son's ability or willingness to communicate with them. Many parents who had previously tried to communicate with their sons regularly and received only monosyllables in response, found that the boy had become more expressive and willing to discuss the trials and tribulations of the day and his successes. Boys do not have to go into a therapy group for this to happen, but in order for communication patterns to change between parents and their sons, it requires some work from the parents. Simply, the daily back and forth of a boy interacting with his peers and debriefing about this with a teacher, or coming home and talking about it with his parents, or discussing it weekly in his youth groups, is a way of helping an adolescent understand his own method of 'doing–being'.

In Brief

- Aggression is an attempt to maintain psychical homeostasis, where the aggressor tries to maintain a coherent image of himself by striking at what threatens him from outside.

- Aggression is a physical response to a physical arousal, which bypasses speech. In bypassing speech, the aggressive act bypasses the codes, reasoning, doubt and ability to wonder that are contained in the act of speaking. A fundamental task with aggressive boys is to assist them to use words rather than fists.

- The capacity for thought and reflection, strong investment in relationships and a belief in their capacity to act seems to separate more capable and successful boys from angrily aggressive boys, in whom these capacities are diminished or absent.

- Aggressive acts are a mix of more or less anger, enjoyment and self-preservation. Not all aggression is angry aggression and some implied aggression is necessary for a boy to survive in the rough and tumble of the school playground or sports field.

- In focusing on the demands and 'bad intentions' of others, aggressive boys leave themselves out. The cure for aggression lies not in helping boys to be more pro-social (that is, putting others first, thinking about others more). Rather, the cure lies in an ethics of self-interest, where an adult helps a boy to gradually understand the problem that the aggression causes for his aims and wishes in life. I call this a 'crisis of possibility'.

- The fundamental aim in helping an aggressive boy is to arrive at a point where—for him—he can act ethically towards what he wants.

- Adolescence involves mastering a paradoxical truth: respecting the law allows a freedom to do as one wishes.

3
The Family: Love, Hate and Anger

People's 'childhood memories' are only consolidated at ... puberty; this involves a complicated process of remodelling, analogous in every way to the process by which a nation constructs legends about its early history.

Sigmund Freud, *Notes Upon a Case of Obsessional Neurosis*

By the time people reach adolescence, they have been 'bathed' in an intricate network of family relationships. In this chapter, I will focus on how these relationships determine, in many subtle and overlapping ways, who adolescents are as people, how they make sense of others and how they react to others.

The shaping of an adolescent is the product of a 'family romance' to which both the child and his parents contribute. The romance is produced within the child's imagination or fantasy, which is constructed upon distortions of the words, actions and deeds of the parents, siblings and wider family members. Freud indicated that puberty is the time when we begin, in a more or less intense manner, to become aware of how our world has shaped us: that is, a version of the 'family romance' becomes conscious. This occurs through adolescents questioning what has been apparent but unspoken throughout their childhood, and making sense of what has happened—in other words, constructing legends about their place in the world.

The arrival of more advanced forms of thought means that an adolescent, rather than accepting more or less passively his place within the family system, begins to imagine other possibilities. Adolescence is a particularly intense time of imaginative activity. Whether these possibilities become probabilities depends on the ingenuity and effort of the adolescent and, in some part, on the nature of the child's relationship with his parents. It is true that by adolescence some important foundations have been laid, but there is much that parents can do to assist their son in his often painful struggle to adulthood.

Chapter 4 will examine the changes and advances (although to many parents these changes hardly seem like advances) of adolescence. These changes can be utilised to assist a boy in moving through adolescence. This chapter explores the importance of family relationships in adolescence, setting the scene for the Doing Anger Differently principles in Part II that a parent of an angry adolescent son can follow.

Douglas's Lost Adolescence

Douglas's father was a prominent and wealthy barrister. He came from a long line of barristers—the type, Douglas told me, who 'earned $100 dollars a word', and whose 'word was law'. Douglas's father had actually wanted to be a physicist, but following a long series of detours through the study of philosophy he eventually submitted to his own father's insistence and became a lawyer, then a barrister. From a young age Douglas had also wanted to be a physicist. When he was a child he had many conversations with his father about the wonders of science.

The Family

Douglas's parents divorced when he was ten. The divorce was precipitated by a financial setback: Douglas's father had been involved in a tax-avoidance scheme that failed and he fell into debt, which seriously limited the family's lifestyle for a time. The parents started arguing continuously. Douglas told me he fell from being the most creative, precious and intelligent child ('no homework was better done than my homework. I was the most intelligent child in my school, according to my parents') to being pushed aside by both parents in their pre- and post-marital struggles. After several years of bitter recriminations between the parents (where Douglas supported his mother), Douglas's father moved in with a girlfriend. Douglas knew the woman—she was a teacher who had taught Douglas at primary school. His mother was outraged by her son's support for his father's new partnership. For some time Douglas continued to live with his mother, who constantly harangued and criticised him, especially when she was drunk. Things reached a point where he could not stand it. His father supported Douglas to live by himself for a short time, but soon withdrew his support due to his financial troubles. In any case, over this time Douglas found his father was remote and distant, preoccupied with other things, and did not want Douglas to be part of his 'new life'. Douglas eventually supported himself—setting up with a friend in a Housing Commission flat while studying his final four years of high school and then university.

Throughout his adolescence and into his adult life he became a loner, moving from friendship group to friendship group with no family to return to. He defined himself in relation to these groups, always very conscious of how he fitted into the group and where he was in the hierarchy, but never making any lasting friendships. Up until the time of his coming to see me, when he was 45, Douglas had been plagued by a relentless need to have the support and recognition of others, as well as a habit of making enemies of those who he thought were his peers.

He did achieve his wish to be a physicist, implanted in him from his early conversations with his father. What is remarkable is that Douglas achieved this despite the setback of his parents' separation: he always ensured he had shelter and a means to continue his studies. It was clear that his early life had deeply rooted in him a desire to succeed, but success came at a cost. Anyone he perceived as a rival in what was a successful academic career in physics (he had been published numerous times in many top international journals) he dealt with in a haze of a punitive rage. He spent enormous amounts of mental energy in fictitious battles with colleagues. Those who did nothing to create enmity with him were dealt with by disparagement in his own mind or by continual avoidance. At other times his rage spilled over into open confrontation. He had been the subject of numerous complaints from his colleagues in the various university departments he had worked in, as he dealt with colleagues at times callously. Interestingly, Douglas's difficulties—of always searching for recognition and dominance—were the source of the excellence in his work.

Douglas was also, unconsciously, on a search for a father. He travelled to and found work within many places around the country and eventually around the globe, each time searching for recognition—from the company boss, professor or head of the university department that he had joined. Douglas felt that such bosses and professors tended to ignore him by collaborating only in a cursory way with his work. This is despite the fact that Douglas needed very little help or guidance on an intellectual level, as evidenced by his publication record and high-standard project work. Alternatively, if not ignored,

The Family

> Douglas felt oppressed by his latest boss, who would be 'too involved' and too directive about his work.

Douglas's adolescence can be considered 'lost' in the sense of the absence of a proper separation being carried out with his family. He continually 'refound' his family—we can find echoes of a yearning for his early familial relations within the relationships he engineered.

How and why does this happen? In the light of this case, I want to take a step back prior to the time of puberty that Freud names as the time of the construction of legends—back to childhood and infancy. This step backwards will allow us to understand more fully the landscape that is being negotiated in adolescence.

It is possible to see infancy and childhood as being a series of a few pivotal moments. From the child's first moments he looks to his caregivers, usually his parents, to satisfy his needs. After these first moments, he also looks to parents and caregivers not just for satisfaction of physical needs, but also for recognition and reassurance: in short, love. Parents and caregivers respond more or less adequately to a child's early needs for sustenance and comfort. After this early time several events occur more or less contemporaneously.

The infant begins to notice that the family is not altogether the ideal, happy, wonderful place that it seemed to be at first. He starts to realise that he is not the centre of his parents' world: the mother does not live up to the impossible task of answering his every need to his satisfaction. This creates questions about the love of the mother. The child sees that his parents are looking beyond him, to something past his own image (an image he has, in fact, only just noticed) and seem to be preoccupied with something else—shopping, work, another child, each other, their social life. It is this something else that leads to the second moment of infancy—childhood.

In this second moment, the child tries to understand and be what it is that his parents (in particular his mother, or whoever is acting in the position of mother) want. There are endless questions, which represent not only an endless curiosity, but also a method of the child trying to 'read between the lines': Where do I fit in? What is wanted of me? How should I be in order to be what my mother/father wants me to be? These questions are less often explicitly asked, but they have their effect in the background of the relation between the child and his parents. Though the parent(s) can answer the explicit questions, they have either only a partial answer, or no answer at all to the implicit questions: these questions the child attempts to answer himself.

For most children, as they grow, this becomes a back-and-forth process between others' wishes for them (parents and their various replacements—grandparents, teachers, coaches, uncles, older brothers) and their own wishes for themselves. What emerges (that is, what a boy ends up 'doing') is something that is neither the boy's own creation, nor the creation of his parents or parental-like guides.

We can imagine such a process in Douglas's case. Douglas states he cannot remember a time when he did not want to be a scientist. Though Douglas's father gave no active command for him to be a physicist, Douglas had both supposed and then adopted his father's wishes through their early discussions about the wonders of science. This 'wish to be' remained a guide throughout his adolescence. The sudden fall from being the 'wonder child' who pleased his parents in every way to being one who was cast aside as the detritus of a failed marriage, was one of the starting points of his difficulties. The tragedy for Douglas, due to his parents' separation and his estrangement from both of them, is that he was not able to enter a dialogue with his father or his mother which might have enabled him to make such wishes his own. The abruptness of Douglas's estrangement from his parents meant he had continued to be caught, well into his adulthood, in a situation of having to suppose a father and attribute wishes or demands from the father figure on himself.

The Family

It is true that most of us never really separate fully from our families, which remain as lifelong presences. Our relations with the figures that we invest our love in as infants and children lay down lifelong methods of investment in our relationships with others. Our family is always present for better or worse, in the manner that we are attracted to, love, use and abuse. However, the point here is not *what* we do—whether we take on our father's or mother's work, or style of relating, or whatever—the point is more *for whom* one does it. Who are we hoping to please when we take a new job, strive for a promotion, face off in a confrontation with a colleague at work, confront another boy in the schoolyard, attempt to be a champion fighter? These questions, 'For whom?' and 'For what reason?' we do things, are crucial.

Douglas was often taking on new directions from outside. In particular he supposed new orders from each new father–professor he implicated in his work. He was always feeling that he had to defend himself from the threats of colleagues who might take this direction from him—perhaps due to the insubstantiality of the direction and the instability of his own image that was based upon this direction. However, each new finding of a 'father' deferred his own search for what he wished to be. 'Performing for others' deafened Douglas to his own wishes. The performance also continued the periodic eruptions of anger and rage that were necessary to keep his image of himself whole. The devastating fall from being the highly valued child to the one who was an outcast, valued by no one, meant that Douglas's life took on a circular structure, with an endless repetition of the same moves within whatever new social and work situations he found himself.

For Douglas, the series of new directions resulted in a lack of direction. He could hold on to his academic career as a success (although he at times abandoned his achievements as worthless). For many boys who become men, such serial switching of direction is ultimately disastrous. Such young men are tossed on the waves of the whims of acquaintances, bosses, gang leaders, fashion ... a sure pathway to despair and anxiety. Being able to find a direction is a guard against anxiety (perhaps not despair, though!). Douglas's case illustrates the importance of parents entering a dialogue with their child about their wishes, goals and plans to assist in the adolescent's separation from them. This dialogue was largely absent in Douglas's life.

I was discussing some paragraphs ago the child's wish-to-be that he takes from his parents, transmitted often unwittingly by the father to the son. The formation of this wish-to-be occurs at the time where the child can begin to participate in an exchange with and manipulation of its world, at the time where he can stand and look triumphantly at his own image in the mirror. At this age—about twelve to eighteen months (although the effects of this moment are lifelong)—the child's image of himself coalesces into a whole. As discussed earlier, we tend to strive for a certain stability in this image, in order to maintain a psychical homeostasis, but the image is always somewhat unstable and requires more or less energy to maintain. It is this image of oneself that is threatened in the case of Alan, or needs to be maintained in the case of John.

Douglas also sought to continually stabilise his self-image in several ways. The rages at the colleagues and the affirmations sought from the father–professors were all attempts to stabilise and bolster his image, in ways similar to John and Alan. But Douglas's image tended to change or flip into a new one periodically and each change of image resulted in a temporary revitalisation. He was always looking to establish the 'new Douglas' in a new context, job or friendship group.

The legends that an adolescent bases on the original family relations from childhood and through adolescence really determine how comfortable he is with his own image—how easily it starts to fragment (as in the case of Alan), and to what degree a boy must seek to stabilise the image (as in the case of Douglas, or John), or must attack his own image (as in the case of Matthew).

I am not saying that what happened to Douglas is necessarily what would have happened to any child in Douglas's situation. On the contrary, the way Douglas as a child made something of his world necessarily bears his own mark. His story is his own construction, his own legend, built on the facts of his history. Perhaps his problem is that he made it too much his own—there was little room for anyone else in his story after the divorce of his parents. Another child might have built a completely different history, one which inspired a very different set of problems.

The process of psychical separation from family occurs slowly through childhood, and reaches its most visible point during adolescence. Many of the problems or achievements of childhood also become very visible in adolescence. It is for this reason that I call adolescence 'childhood made manifest'. The events and dramas of family life up to this point are organised, consciously or unconsciously, into a means of acting for the adolescent. These 'legends' are formed mutually, by both parents and their adolescent son: this stresses the importance of the parental input in adolescence.

Douglas's case shows how the vagaries of separation, as they are played out in adolescence, are particularly important. If childhood is a time of construction, adolescence is a time of reconstruction. Adolescence gives a 'second chance' at a making of the individual.

Parents

It is probably clear, from what I have written so far, that mothers and fathers have quite distinct roles to play in regard to the raising of boys. However, this is not so clear in practice. With the rise of fragmented and single-parent families, many mothers come to play a type of father role with their sons, and with intact families, many fathers participate in motherhood roles from their children's births.

Though the parenting practices of mothers and fathers are becoming more mixed, one can speak of times when fathering and mothering are important and called for. Add to this the fact that mothers can call up the name of busy ('Wait till your father gets home!') and absent or dead ('What would your father think of that?') fathers to the child. Also, children's fantasies about their origins often invoke absent fathers and mothers. The situation becomes far more complex than a simple reduction to a biological definition of parenthood.

It is perhaps more accurate to think of the mother and father as positions, or functions, rather than inextricably linked to their biological roles. When I use the term 'mother' and 'father' in this book I generally mean the one who functions, acts or is put in the place of a mother or father—which is most often the biological parent. This point may seem esoteric, but it has important implications for the functioning of fragmented families and enables parents to act in ways that they may not believe possible. I'll discuss this under the principles for parents in Chapter 7 but first I'll outline the importance and problems of the mothering and fathering positions.

I also deal below with the issue of hatred and anger within the family, and its origins within the family relations. There is nearly always a degree of ambivalence in the relationship between a son and his parents. By ambivalence I mean the seemingly opposing tendencies of both love and hate are called up at regular intervals within the interactions between the son and his parents. The nature and genesis of this ambivalence is different in the case of the relation with a mother as opposed to the relation to a father.

Mothers

One day I was running a Doing Anger Differently group at a high school. The conversation turned to mothers. The tone of the conversation in the group quickly moved to a discussion about loss, which surprised me, because it was only the third meeting of the

The Family

group, which contained several bullies. We had been talking about what made members of the group angry. Daniel, a tall muscular boy, suddenly started to talk about how his mother had died when he was nine years old. He said that anyone who said anything bad about his mother would be 'smashed' by him. Other boys in the group also recounted the loss of their maternal figures.

One boy, Lindsay, summed up the discussion when he said, 'Well, guys, it just shows how we are all mummy's boys in the end ...' This group articulated a problem for boys: the loss of their relation with their mother. Daniel had only a dim memory of his mother, but it was a memory he carried with him every day in the schoolyard.

Now, most boys do not have to endure the sudden loss of mother figures as the boys in this group had. However, the suddenness of the losses illustrates a point. The mother often represents a time (most probably a mythical time) where the boy was cared for and nurtured and was at the centre of a universe, a place he is displaced from gradually if all goes smoothly. The problem for many of the boys in this group is that they were seeking to recapture being the centre of the universe in one way or another through their relationships with others.

Daniel had preserved the memory of his mother as an all-nurturing and caring individual. Anyone who insulted or challenged that image was dealt with physically—in a similar way to how Alan attempted to destroy his persecutors. Daniel said that he felt that his mother was the only person who really knew him, and cared for him. Part of the problem was perhaps Daniel's rather harsh and punitive father, who had no room to allow a nurturing and accommodating relationship with his son. What Daniel didn't have at home, he made sure existed amongst his peers at school. Everyone knew not to step 'out of line' with Daniel: if you wanted to be his friend, you had to do things exactly how he liked it. There was no compromise. He was a 'pure individual' without acknowledgement of the needs of others. This was demonstrated rather dramatically one therapy session, where it

The Problem

had been pointed out clearly to Daniel the futility of his aggression, in that it often destroyed what he said he wanted: friends he could trust. He became angrier and angrier with me as we discussed this until he bent over, cupped his hands over his ears and yelled repetitively, 'I'm not listening to you any more!' Daniel was not ready to face the contradiction between wanting friends he could trust and having these friends do exactly as he wanted. As well as preserving the loss of his mother, Daniel avenged this loss on a daily basis: by making all his acquaintances bow to his every need.

Daniel had invented a mother that was still with him in a way, whom he couldn't mourn and thus move on to more fulfilling relationships. In many ways he continued to act like a nine year old (and a young one at that) who had lost the love of his mother, and everyone had to treat him as if it were so. His invented mother had trapped him in a past he had difficulty moving beyond.

This is exactly how many boys with problems of anger and aggression act: as if the world is the lost mother, as if everyone should bow to the aggressive boy's needs, wishes and wants. They appear to be very self-centred and demanding, prepared to use force to get their way. There is no bending to or accommodation of others' wishes. These boys practise a sort of lopsided, one-way justice, where they position themselves as the 'poor me' in any situation.

Recall the importance of the mother in responding to the child's needs and wants. Of course, mothers do this more or less well. There is necessarily a time when the mother looks beyond the child and this involves a loss. A boy cannot expect to have his every need or whim catered for into adulthood, and the time must come when he separates from the mother. This is a loss which any boy suffers in childhood, and it is somewhat normal for a boy to seek some form of unconscious restitution for this loss, throughout the reminder of his life. However, the losses of the boys in the group were magnified due to the suddenness of the loss.

My point—so well summed up by Lindsay—is that the loss of the mother is on the horizon of much of the destructive anger and aggression that we see amongst youth. Boys find something lacking, empty or not to their liking in the world or amongst the people that populate it. This loss is turned outwards, onto the world, which they see as full of persecution from ill-meaning people. Nothing can measure up to the time of the mother, now lost, and many boys seek to preserve this time through an expectation that all will fit around them. Commonly, many boys act in a physical way to ensure their expectations are met, which brings censure from school and family authorities. Acting on this expectation often means acting towards their own detriment, as a boy fails to understand why others will not accommodate his needs. We find here the tendency of many angry people, who recurrently see the world as a problem, and that it is the world that should change.

This loss of a mother can often be turned inwards as well. The tendency then is to find the world poor and empty, which in turn easily collapses into a tendency to find oneself poor and empty. It was perhaps this collapse that Daniel was defending against with his 'I'm not listening to you!' once he had encountered the futility of his aggression. This is why we find self-destructiveness and depression are so often associated with anger and aggression. There is a strong link between anger, sadness and a boy's maternal bond.

Fathers

The loss of the close connection with a mother is precipitated by several factors. Perhaps the first of these is the development of the child's ability to speak. As the child substitutes a cry with speech and language (which includes gesture and facial expressions), the reliance on the mother's ability to respond by 'reading' the child, by guessing what he wants, is lessened. Speech is a move away from the purely inchoate level of utterance based on physical need to an articulation in words of what is left over after the physical need is satisfied: the wish for love and recognition. Speech inserts itself between the child and the mother. The child must now place its needs in speech, which is to express its internal world in a system developed by others. This is the first, perhaps most fundamental step, of the child accommodating to another. It is one reason why aggressive boys prefer physical force over speech to get what they want. In using words, they may only approximate what they want: which is another loss. In the moment of persecution, the use of force meets an internal need for revenge or destruction of the other far more adequately than mere words.

At its simplest, this intervention between the mother and the child, into the demand for and satisfaction of need by another, is the role of the father. The father 'inserts' himself between the mother and the child. However, this intervention by the father has a dual function. It is a well-worn idea that boys need a father to be a role model, to show a boy how to be a man. In the normal run of things, this is exactly what happens: the little boy idealises the father and wants to be like him. The father is the strongest and wisest of men. We have already seen in the case of Douglas how the lost wish of the father to be a scientist was taken up by the son. In this sense the father can lie at the base of a boy's 'wish-to-be' in addition to helping facilitate the ambition when the appropriate time comes.

As well as quantities of love, hate can also be aroused in sons on account of the father. The seeds of hatred are sown in the sons taking up the direction of their father. It is important for the son to not only take up the father's wish, but 'to go beyond the father' in making the wish his own. This 'going beyond' necessarily involves some distortion, improvement, modification or gain that the son builds on what he sees his father had. Rejection and overcoming is fundamental to the process of a son coming into his own, and is discussed further in cases below.

The Family

A second part of the father function is that of prohibition. The father shows a boy what is and is not allowed. This founds a boy's respect for the fundamental social rules of society, a respect that is not necessarily brought forth within the maternal bond.

I was once invited to speak at a community violence forum by a state member of parliament. A remarkable thing happened in the discussion afterwards. The debate became one of whether it was justifiable to use violence against those boys who were violent. I had made the point that to use violence to stop violence was simply to use the same method that caused the problem in the first place. One man in the audience yelled at this point, 'Give 'em a bunch of fives, and that will teach those violent ringleaders what to do'. His words were greeted with cheers by at least half of the audience. It seemed breathtaking that community members who had turned up to an anti-violence forum were advocating violence to solve the problem!

However, on reflection, I think those people do have a point. Many boys, including those same boys who grieved the loss of their mothers, have not found a way to limit their demands of the world, or find a way to get what they want within the normal rules of society. There is a certain violence—by this I don't mean physical violence—in the 'No!' of the father. The father's role is to indicate to a boy: 'You can do this, but not that'. He shows a boy that he must act within the rules of society. The problem is that the father cannot be a law unto himself, using violence to fight violence, as then boys only aspire to become the violent father, one who has shown himself to be outside and above the law.

The father has a two-fold function: to prohibit certain things and to unite this prohibition with the wishes of a boy. In doing this, the father turns the boy towards the world and shows him how to deal with its difficulties. This function continues to hold its importance through the pivotal moment of adolescence.

Other Fathers

A boy, particularly an adolescent boy, can have several 'fathers', not just the biological one. As a boy looks outwards from his family towards the wider world, many possible father figures may provide an orientation for him. This brings to mind a 15-year-old boy, Greg, who was referred to me.

> Greg declared that he knew that one day he was going to get a criminal record, although he didn't want to. He told me how all his uncles and his father had criminal records and it was inevitable that this fate would befall him.
>
> Greg also talked about a teacher, Mr Warren, who was 'able to teach us even though we did not want to learn'. Mr Warren succeeded because Greg felt that the teacher understood him. He had told Mr Warren that he wanted to become a qualified mechanic and work on high-performance cars. A problem had arisen—for Greg and for his school—when Mr Warren went on a term's sabbatical leave. The emergency teacher, Ms McLean, whose fate it was to replace the much-loved teacher, was in Greg's view, 'a bitch' who didn't care about him. She just put the schoolwork on the board and expected him to do it. She had been reduced, for Greg, to the function of merely passing on knowledge, and had failed to inspire in him the desire for knowledge. When Ms McLean asked Greg what he wanted to be, he had replied, 'A dole cheat'.

What factor made the difference here? The measure of love and respect that Greg had for Mr Warren and not for Ms McLean. The two teachers could perhaps teach in exactly the same manner but Mr Warren was a more effective teacher for Greg, *because of how Greg thought of Mr Warren*. Greg's relationship to Mr Warren had some potential to help him evade the fate of criminality.

In popular language, Mr Warren was able to act as a 'father figure' to Greg. This is a phenomenon that increasingly happens as boys progress through adolescence—they look outside the family for substitute fathers. Mr Warren could act as a substitute father but Ms McLean could not, and Greg could not overcome his numerous problems with learning with Ms McLean, who was subjected to considerable insults by him. This substitution of parental figures is dealt with further, in the discussion below of the case study of Andrew and Peter.

The Function of a Father

How did Mr Warren come to be a father figure? How might his functioning as a father assist Greg? There are numerous 'mentoring' and 'leadership' programs across the country that aim to install a 'father figure' in a boy's life. The theory lying behind these (often not very well thought out) is that the original father is absent or has failed to provide the adequate mix of showing and prohibition required of a father. But it is a relatively normal part of adolescent development, perhaps even an essential one, that other 'fathers' figure in a boy's life.

At the time that I met Greg he was in the process of constructing his own 'family legend'. He had become discontented with the narrowness of his family's life. Part of the 'family legend' he did not like: the serial convictions and time in gaol. The only model within his family was one of transgression of the law and gaol. He said clearly, 'I do not want this'. His problem was that he did not know how to evade the fate. Mr Warren offered a way, even though it was difficult: 'You can learn and become a qualified mechanic, even though it will require work'. This is the first essence of the function of a father: you must do this, even though you find it difficult. And also: 'Although it is difficult, I have done it, and I will show you how to do it'. This is the demonstration of a way. It includes positive assistance with what

Greg wanted as well as a negative function: you cannot do *that* if *this* is what you want.

Other social structures can act as a type of father: a school, a social friendship group or a youth gang, for example. This is why the friendship group is so important in adolescence. The identification with a group, the rush for sameness, and the adolescent's trajectory away from the family can easily combine to lead a boy astray.

The Child's Internal Family

All this gives no guarantee of how the child will be affected by his mother and father. The child produces a fantasy of his parents, a legend or an individual myth in adolescence. There is not a direct causal relation between an individual's history and 'how they have turned out', although this is how it appears to the individual.

> Jeff, a 25-year-old man, told me once that his father came to visit him after not having seen him for many years. He had been quite scared of his father, who left his family when Jeff was eight, although he retained few actual memories of him. Most of his ideas about his father were based on stories transmitted through members of his maternal family, who had said things like 'I never liked your father', and 'He was a big, tough man, not scared to tell everyone what he thought'. Jeff's mother had said, 'When your father said something, that was that. There was no changing his view and that's how things would go.' Jeff had had problems with anxiety, which he often pitched as a battle to be his father: 'My father wouldn't be scared in this situation'.
>
> Jeff went with his father to a popular boating lake, where sailboats were passing. His father looked at the boats and tried to figure out which type and how old they were. Jeff thought,

The Family

> 'You have been away so long and there is so much to talk about and you just look at the boats ...'

The story shows that Jeff's real father was nothing like the father he held inside him. Jeff's real father paled beside the one he battled to be—tough, fierce and uncompromising. It is the child's internal family, the one that has been fashioned as a result of his family history and the legends he has constructed from it, that determine how he behaves, when he will be angry and when he will be aggressive. The internal family may be important to understand if one is to understand an angry boy's often counterproductive and self-destructive behaviour.

It is also therefore unlikely that single acts of parents, or single traumatic events (excepting of course major traumas which result in permanent losses, as in the case of Daniel's mother, or the divorce of Douglas's parents) will have a lasting impact. Rather it is the ongoing nature of relations within a family that make the man.

A further point: in working with a troubled adolescent it is not the past that is worked with, but how a boy makes sense of himself, which may be more or less an effect of how a boy makes sense of his past. These are all activities very much rooted in the present and can be changed by events within the present.

Parental Responses

So, what then can parents do? What are some appropriate parental responses to what often seems like the storm of adolescence? Two cases below—the response of a mother and a father respectively—illustrate the difficulties of responding to adolescent problems, while Chapter 7 contains general principles that parents can use in responding to their angry and out-of-control children.

David and Anne: The Mother as Father

Recall the case of Anne and her son David. Anne had told me that although David was intelligent and liked going to school, his grades had been falling and he had lost direction since Year 7. David's father, a university lecturer who saw his son every other weekend, would fly into a rage about his son's non-academic attitude to schoolwork. David's father wished him to go to university, while Anne wanted David to 'do whatever would make him happy'.

In terms of the functions of mothers and fathers I discussed earlier, Anne's response is a mother's response. Nurturing and caring, Anne just wants what is best for 'her boy'. Anne told me that she was not going to do to her son what her father had done to her, which was to prohibit her from doing what she really loved, nursing. She wanted her son to do whatever he wanted. Although Anne complained continually about her own father's prohibition, she had, in fact, made good use of the prohibition: having a successful career as a doctor's secretary, eventually moving to an important administrative post in a university department of medicine. Through her son, Anne was trying to right a perceived past wrong enacted on her by her father. It was as if she were saying, 'This was done to me, so I will do the opposite to my son'. However, it was far from clear that what Anne's father had 'done' to her was 'all bad', and that what Anne was saying to her son was 'all good'. A parent's own past can be an important guide to raising his or her own child. However, Anne's son seemed to be asking for guidance, a request she couldn't hear because of her own history.

The problem with Anne's response was that it gave David no ideas about how to define what he would like to do, and certainly no means to achieve it. This is a very different response from that of Mr Warren, Greg's teacher, who was able to indicate a direction and the means to achieve it. Unfortunately, David could not recognise

The Family

his father's wish that he go to university as one he wanted to take up. This left him with little support or guidance in the transition from childhood to adulthood.

There is nothing wrong, in itself, with parents wanting something for their children. The separation of a child from his or her family is neither totally the child's doing, nor totally the parents' doing. It is an act made from both sides. The problem with David's parents' responses is that his mother left it completely to David to decide on his wishes (despite his request for help), whereas his father ignored his son in attempting to impose his own wishes. A cooperative building of a future requires that, at a crucial time of separation, parents be active in their responses to their child's requests for guidance.

One of the factors that lay behind Anne's 'I just want you to be happy' was her fear of losing her son. The maternal fear of losing the closeness with her son meant she could not be a father and help him separate. She wished that the intimate bond she had with David could remain. She feared a catastrophic end to their relationship where David would leave and live full-time with his father. All this created obstacles for David to overcome in his separation: if a mother clings to her child, still trying to answer his every need into adolescence, it makes his painful task of separation all the more painful. It is a difficulty that many mothers have spoken to me about, particularly those who do the majority of the parenting of the children, with the father partially or completely absent.

How does one 'let go' of a son and help him turn to the world? Anne solved this problem in a manner that was somewhat bewildering to David. At times she tried to keep him very close—often precisely at those times when he was being independent. At other times Anne pushed him away, often at those times when David was returning to her for comfort. This problem—when to nurture and when to encourage a son's independence—is taken up again in Part II.

The Problem

Anne also complained that David was 'a chip off the old block': becoming a copy of his father—irritable and at times explosive. Anne had told me what had attracted her to David's father was that he 'needed looking after'. She also became caught up in the care of David after his birth (as is natural for any mother) as he was very sickly, and she found it difficult to let go of this caring role once her son became more vigorous. In many ways Anne was replicating her relationship with her husband with her son. It did not occur to Anne that she was placing her son in a certain position in relation to her. In the absence of Anne stepping back a little, David was beginning to be angry and aggressive in an attempt to force her to keep her distance. It is painful for a mother to acknowledge that it is time to step back from the looking after, and step forward in another way.

However, a mother can invoke the father's function. Even when she is acting as a single mother, struggling at times to provide for her son, it is possible for a mother to be father-like, having an ongoing dialogue with the son. A father, whilst indicating a direction, unites what he wants for his son with some indication of what the son has signified he wants—by his actions, his pastimes, what he enjoys. This invariably involves spending some time with the son, talking and doing things together. The son absorbs something from a father at many levels: in conversation (as in the case of Douglas), in shared activity, and through the son witnessing and hearing about what the father has achieved.

Peter and Andrew: Rejection is Not Failure

> Peter, a 15 year old, and his father Andrew came to see me one day over a fight they had had over Peter's mountain bike. Helen, Peter's mother, had called me and asked me to see them as they had almost come to blows. Peter had returned home upset after he had taken his repaired, second-hand bike to the

The Family

> bike track, and another father had pulled him aside and told him that his bike was set up wrongly. Peter had told his father that his work on the bike was 'wrong, wrong, wrong'. Andrew said he was not going to speak to his son or help him on any of his projects until he apologised. Helen was finding it very difficult to live in the house with two warring males.

It took just two meetings with me for Andrew and Peter to resolve their differences about the bike. However, the conflict had opened something for both Peter and Andrew which was important but difficult to discuss. The case is an example of how a son's rejection of his father can be wounding; how the father responds to the rejection can be quite decisive for the son.

In Peter's eyes, his father had fallen from the all-knowing, wise figure of his childhood, when his father taught him to play golf, to sail and to ski. The conflict over the bike signified (although Peter could not immediately articulate this) that he, as the son, had begun to find his own path, separate from the father. The rejection of the father's word is important in this process.

The forsaking of the parents and the valorisation of substitute figures can be an important aspect of adolescence. This requires the parent to sustain the loss of his or her child, even if it is a temporary one. It is a necessary advance away from the family and into the world for the adolescent. In many ways, substitute parents are an attempt to re-activate the lost parents of infancy in all their might and glory. We often find in the substitute or 'new' father some familiar aspects of the original one. For example, in the case of Greg, Mr Warren had first qualified as a mechanic and later became a teacher. This was an echo of Greg's own father and uncles, all of whom spent hours fixing cars (an activity that Greg had presumably witnessed much of when he was young), but who were not qualified. In this way, Greg found in Mr Warren a means of 'going beyond the father'. It should not be forgotten that the search for and glorification of other figures who 'know it all' is a compliment, an unconscious homage from the adolescent to the original parent.

The Guarantee of Parental Failure

Sigmund Freud relates a story of an acquaintance, a mother who asked him for advice on how to raise her child so that she would not make mistakes and end up being a failure as a parent. Freud responded with characteristic frank bleakness: 'Don't worry, no matter what you do you will fail'. His comment can be taken in two ways. First, that in the child's eyes it is necessary that the parent falls from his high place of an idealised being to become a common, everyday human. As I have already said, this requires recognition on the part of the child of his parent's faults and failures. Second, this statement could be taken as meaning that no matter what the parents actually do, no matter how perfect they attempt to be as parents, they will end up failing. Indeed, the modern malaise of the search for parenting perfection can be the creation of a private hell for a child, one in which there is no place for the parent to fail, become human and commonplace and thus to allow the child to take up his own place in the world.

Parents who are somewhat secure in themselves, who are able to take the pain of being 'knocked down' by their children, can provide this place best. It is the father who is modest and calm about his achievements, rather than grandiose and extravagant, who makes room for his son to build a place for his own achievements.

In Brief

- By adolescence, children have been immersed in a family romance that has functioned as a fundamental reference point. During adolescence the family ceases to be the only emotional universe and other possibilities are imagined.

The Family

- In childhood there is an alienation from a mythical pre-verbal state when all the physical and emotional needs of the child are met by a mother. It occurs at a time when the child has begun to form a coherent image of himself.
- This starts a process of separation that continues through adolescence and into adulthood. The separation from the family of origin is often unstable, provisional and never complete. Adolescence is a crucial time in this process of separation, where the boy moves from being a child to envisioning and establishing a life of his own.
- How parents think about and interact with their son can have a crucial effect on this process of separation in adolescence.
- The recurrent 'It's not fair' and victim-hood involved in anger can be seen as a problem of separation. Anger and aggression can emerge from the shadow of an unresolved maternal bond, in that they are a demand that the world change and give way to a boy's wishes. This is often in the absence of a boy developing a vision of what he wants for his own life and the means to achieve this vision.
- The father is crucial in the boy's separation from the family. The father can both indicate a direction and make a prohibition that limits the boy's 'fun'. This dual role enables a boy to work, rather than only enjoy.
- The roles of mother and father are less tied to the actual biological mother and father and can be seen as functions—functions that can be fulfilled by other people.
- The historical events of a family give no guarantee of how a child will be affected. The 'family romance' is an individual one, created on actual historical events but dependent on the 'take' that a boy has on these events. This means that parents are working not with the past, but with how a boy makes sense of himself, which is an activity of the present.

- Parenting in adolescence is a delicate balance of giving guidance to a boy, as well as stepping back to allow a boy to find his own way. Part of this may be a boy finding influences from outside the family that are 'better' than those inside the family.
- All of this is aimed at helping a boy achieve a vision for what he wants, and having the means to follow what he wants, inside the rules and laws of society.

4
The Age of Adolescence

The human individual has to devote himself to the great task of detaching himself from his parents, and not until that task is achieved can he cease to be a child and become a member of the social community.

Freud, *Introductory Lectures*

As outlined in the previous chapter, the reordering that takes place at puberty is based on the bedrock of the family's loves, limits, prohibitions, freedoms and relationships—in short, the family romance of childhood. At the same time, adolescence is a time of rewriting, when new lines can be written over old. The primary means of this is through the adolescent's expanding social horizons. Adolescence is the middle epoch of the three epochs of an individual: child, adolescent and adult. Of the three, adolescence is perhaps the most dynamic, concerned with the ordering and remodelling of the experiences of childhood, and a striving towards, and imagining of, a future. Parents, teachers and other professionals can make a profound difference at this time.

In considering the influence of adults on adolescents, it is useful to ask: What is it, exactly, that goes on in adolescence? What is the substance of the changes? What can influence these developments?

Adolescence as a Developmental Turning Point

Adolescence is a cultural construct built on the biological changes of puberty. The overt signs of sexual maturity give a clear indication of the onset of adolescence. To many parents, the idea that the stress and storm of adolescence is a direct result of these biological changes is a seductive one. However, biological factors appear to interact with social and mental factors, and these social and mental factors are influenced by an adolescent's social environment.

Social and mental factors include the demand for independence, the fact of sexual maturity, newly acquired abilities in abstract thought, and a search for an identity. Though these factors are commonly associated with a rise in the influence of the social group and a lessening in the influence of parents, parents remain important, both in terms of what they say and do, and also *in absentia*, through the adolescent's internal family. Adolescence can be characterised as a period of conflict between family and peer values, and this conflict brings about much of the stress and storm of adolescence.

How adolescents negotiate and struggle with these conflicts has important results. This is because such adolescent conflicts are associated with a particularly intense period of intellectual and moral development and the development of a sense of identity. Adolescence is, for many, a world in preparation for the adult world: a moratorium where physical and mental abilities begin to approximate adult abilities, without the expectation that these abilities be put to full use in employment and procreation. Though there is an element of 'trying it out' in the adolescent world, difficulties in these years pose many risks for adult life, as what is being tried out may coalesce into an adult identity. Parents and others in contact with young adolescents are in an important position to shape and influence the adolescent's mental, emotional, personal and moral development.

The Overlapping Spheres of Influence in Adolescence

Several spheres of influence overlap to a greater or lesser degree, and thus determine the path of an adolescent. These are, in no particular order, the family, peers and friends, school and teachers. Each has it own place and variable degree of influence over any particular adolescent. Typically, secondary school serves as a transition place, where an adolescent moves from being influenced almost entirely by family to being influenced more strongly by peers. However, the family tends to retain a life-long role (despite ceasing to be as present physically) due to the family's foundational character. I dealt substantially with the influence of parents in the previous chapter, and I will discuss here the influence of peers and the adolescent group.

Peers, groups and playing at making reality

Friends are a boy's primary mode of social expression. The group is the place where an adolescent boy starts to enact and discover his own particular way of viewing the world. As such it has a peculiarly powerful influence. I'll give here a few examples of the power of adolescent groups from my clinical work.

Outsiders

I worked with a number of aggressive boys in a school that had had a problem with a series of very violent incidents. The incidents were a reflection of a problematic culture within the school, with a high level of disobedience and aggression, which in itself was a reflection of a high level of poverty, domestic and communal violence, and unemployment within the local community. The group of boys had had a series of ups and downs that were quite dramatic, but had resulted in them bonding together quite strongly. There had been several breathtakingly honest moments of examination of the problems of anger and aggression in their lives, perpetrated by themselves and others. As the group's sessions drew to a close, the boys began to talk about how to finish the group, and made some plans.

On the final day, when the boys walked into the room where the group was held, a video of a film was playing. *Cool Runnings* is about a team of initially inept Jamaicans competing against impossible odds in the Olympic bobsleigh event. All the boys insisted that despite their well-made plans, to end the group they wished to watch the film together. This was despite the fact that they had all seen the film previously. Grudgingly, I let them watch it, unable to comprehend their interest, muttering to my co-therapist that it seemed a disappointing way to end the sessions.

Six months later, I returned to interview the boys from this group individually. When one came into the room as another was leaving, they would both jump into the air and slap hands, singing 'We are the members of the bobsleigh team'. Whilst I thought nothing of it initially, when it happened in the third change of interviews I remembered the film viewing in the final session. It dawned on me: the boys had used the narrative from the film in order to express their common bonds. This is what drew them to the film in the final session of the group, despite having seen it previously.

I also remembered the final weeks of the group, were we had discussed how the boys were going to use what they had discovered in the group outside in the school grounds. The boys had raised many problems to do with 'looking like you're tough', 'not letting your guard down', and what to do when 'someone steps up to fight you'. Together they had worked out several ways to stop someone from challenging them in the first place. One had been to help each other with what I had insisted on in the first week of the group—that no violence occur in the group. Over time the group had internalised this ideal.

So the boys, now outsiders in a somewhat violent subculture of a school, were trying to survive as a group. They had adopted a film of outsiders sticking together as a sort of filmic motif, so that in the school grounds they might maintain the group they had created once the formal group had finished. This is a dramatic demonstration of how groups can shape what does and does not get expressed and acted upon within adolescence.

The metaphor of the bobsleigh team had given the boys a term around which to keep alive the parts of themselves that they had discovered in their group work. It allowed them to maintain a level of psychic bonding, and thus the ideals and aims they had developed, once the group had finished.

The anger show

I and my co-therapist were working with a group of five adolescent boys referred for behavioural and emotional difficulties—mainly to do with anger. We spoke in the group for some time about their experiences of anger and how these influenced the boys' lives. However, the process had been rather difficult: the boys found it annoying and had been unfocused whenever the discussion about anger came up in the group—inevitably brought up by the therapists. The group was stuck, unable to find a way to allow boys to speak of the difficulties that had led to their involvement in the group.

The therapy was being videotaped. All the boys had carefully positioned themselves with their backs to the video—there had been much suspicion and fear regarding the camera, as to why it was there, who would watch it, and the like. Without hope, I asked the boys about anger. A boy volunteered that he had been in a fight. I then asked the other boys to assist in interviewing. The boy who was about to be interviewed suggested that he should be facing the camera. From that moment on, a profound change occurred in the group.

The boys rapidly agreed to 'do a talk show': setting up a stage, improvising a microphone, arguing with each other as to who would be interviewed first. They established a central, organising metaphor, through which they were able to speak about themselves for the remainder of the group's life. The game became named *The Jerry Springer Show* and boys positioned the whiteboard as a screen from behind which guests entered, stools were placed on boxes in the set, the lights were dimmed. To ensure the game remained an expressive parody, a boy played a heavy metal CD as the first guest entered. Some boys chanted, 'Jerry, Jerry'. There was a problem: Jerry was nowhere to be found. The boys attempted to force each other into this role but no one was willing to take it up. Clearly an invitation had been issued; initially reluctantly, then enthusiastically, I joined the game, interviewing boys about their difficulties with anger and with other people.

Over weeks, the metaphor was adapted and reshaped. I became the interlocutor to whom boys were able to speak of their difficulties, but had the safety of the game to retreat to when things became too difficult. The moment the group commenced playing the talk show game, the camera's function in the group likewise underwent a profound change, from an oppressive instrument of surveillance—by the school and parents—to a field of play, where the boys were suddenly free to not be themselves, to try other roles and act. Paradoxically, this convention of being not-self allowed participants in the game to gain knowledge of themselves, to become themselves more fully. Only by 'unselfing the self' could the boys discover more about themselves.

Celebrating being other
Another group I conducted had a celebratory moment. The group was held in a drama room, where there was a cupboard full of dress ups. The group had been one that formed relatively quickly, with the six members rapidly moving to reveal quite difficult and intimate problems about their lives. About halfway through the group's scheduled sessions, the boys decided to descend on the dress-up cupboard. At first, they chose relatively conventional costumes. They then became more and more outrageous, donning women's hats, gloves and, finally, women's dresses. The more outrageous the dresses became, the more gleeful the boys' reactions became.

What became clear was that the safer the boys became in the group, the more they were able to play with being something or someone else, in a manner that would have met with strong disapproval from their peers in the playground. The adolescent group provided the means to play at crossing one of the most fundamental divides of adolescence, that of gender. In playing this game, a fundamental question is asked: What is a man? It is a question that some boys answer via their peers through participating in an aggressive hierarchy in their adolescent group.

In groups adolescents are able to play, using metaphors to experiment and discover things beyond themselves and beyond their families. In not being themselves in such groups, adolescents extend themselves. This is the enormous power of the adolescent group. As such, groups serve a very important function for the separation of adolescence.

These examples are illustrations of how adolescents use play to extend themselves and their sense of who they are. It is the process I call 'doing–being', in that the boy's activity (doing) in a group both defines and extends who he is (being). Understanding this process is important if one is to work successfully with adolescents.

The Aggressive Power of the Group

> When I was at John's school, he introduced me to a younger friend, Bob. 'Bob needs help. He's getting into trouble with the teachers all the time', John told me.
>
> Bob was a small, wiry boy, with a baseball cap on backwards. 'Why are you getting into trouble, Bob?' I asked.
>
> 'I just get really angry and I go off,' Bob replied in a monotone.
>
> 'What happens when you go off?'
>
> 'I feel like punching someone or yelling and swearing.'

The Problem

> 'Yeah,' said John, 'I heard from Chip the other day what happened on Saturday. Man, you must have really taken that guy apart. I heard he was heaps bigger than you as well. Chip said you just decked him! Everyone around here has been saying what a champion fighter you are.'
>
> I had been watching Bob while John was speaking. Initially he looked down, hanging his head, only glancing up. He then smiled and, enlivened, said, 'Yeah, I bet no one in Year 7 will fight me anymore when they hear about that.'
>
> John turned to me and said, 'The guy he decked was in Year 9! Can you believe that? He knocked him down, even though he was two years older than him!'

Such is the problem confronting aggressive boys at school. By agreeing to come along with John to meet me, Bob acknowledged there was a problem, but John steered the conversation immediately to glorifying Bob's aggression. John had tried a similar move in a group session when describing his role in an attack on another boy. I knew John was the leader of a group of boys, and Bob was beginning to join their group, membership of which seemed to do with fighting abilities.

Boys as permeable to the outside world as Alan (see Chapter 1) often require a group of peers that can somehow ground, or shore up, their unstable and changeable sense of self. Adolescents look to others to share and legitimise their actions. The process of developing separate beliefs, identities and an independent life from the family of origin is important and emotionally difficult for boys. There are often high levels of conflict between the codes laid out by the family and the paths suggested by the actions and attitudes of peers.

Boys with particularly aggressive and coercive relationship patterns may find this process even more difficult than usual, as they may commonly be rejected at school due to their aggression.

The Age of Adolescence

An aggressive reputation can be difficult to change, as peers tend to respond aggressively to peers who they know are aggressive.

In the examples above, the peer groups help the boys develop a sense of individuality: being with friends and playing extends the adolescent's sense of self. However, the opposite is common in groups of aggressive peers, the so-called youth gang. Often the group is controlled by the most aggressive and ruthless member, and the hierarchy in the group is ordered according to who has the most aggressive status. Rather than differentiation, such a group is based on sameness: boys in the group aspire to an aggressive, violent ideal, often based on or around the traits of a leader.

I also worked with a group of boys who collectively told me the story of Bungo at the beginning of their group.

> Bungo was apparently a fellow who didn't work, but lived by a lake and spent his time out at the front of his house drinking, smoking and talking to his friends who dropped around. Bungo had his share of problems, according to the group. His wife had left him and he no longer saw his three children, who lived with his wife in another state. The boys admired Bungo because he just didn't care what others thought of him. One boy told the group that once, one of Bungo's friends told Bungo that a convicted sex offender had moved into his street. Bungo went to see the offender to straighten him out. He started assaulting the sex offender 'no questions asked' and the police were called. When the police arrived, Bungo dealt with the police officer in a similar manner and then returned to continue assaulting the offender.

The mythical status of this story was confirmed by the boy who introduced the story: 'A friend of my brother knows that guy Bungo and …' Nonetheless, the story outlines an ideal to which many of the members of the group aspired: to be the violent man, outside the law, a law unto himself, a man who takes the law into his own hands. Such ideals form the basis of the sameness to which the members of rejected and violent groups of boys aspire. Difference is often not tolerated and individuals are excluded or punished for any difference (be it skin colour, sexuality, physical strength—the characteristic is often somewhat arbitrary). Bungo, although none of the group members had actually met him, formed an imaginary paternal figure to the group. I started to use the figure of Bungo in sessions when boys described certain actions, in order to provoke discussion: 'What would Bungo think about that?' 'What would Bungo do in that situation?' 'What do you all think about what Bungo would have done?' 'Would you do something differently to what Bungo did?' This was a way of questioning the ideal of violence to which many of the group members aspired. Such role models are rarely spoken about explicitly, and one of my tasks in this group of boys was to help them start thinking about the ideal of 'best fighter', to which some of them aspired. All of this has much to do with the task of reorganising the field of enjoyment for each boy, a matter I discuss further in Part II.

As shown by Bob's change in demeanour in his meeting with me, this aggressive, outside-the-law ideal has the function of assuaging his negative feelings about himself. John's congratulatory introduction appeared to erase Bob's concerns about the difficulties that his aggression and anger caused, and allowed him to take pleasure in the portrayal of his fighting abilities. There is nothing wrong with a boy feeling enjoyment but (as I found out later) Bob's aggression, which he used to sustain this view of himself in front of his peers, was causing him multiple difficulties at school and at home, as well as with the police. Bob's aggression allowed him to belong to a hierarchy, to have his place, on the condition that he acted on and professed to the same ideals of aggression as his peers.

How does this aggressive group membership work within an individual's mind? It is not a case of simple learning or copying the aggression and an angry style of self-expression. Rather, such 'falling in' with a group of peers *involves a boy drawing an unconscious inference* when he meets a like-minded boy. It is as if he says, 'I am the same as you, therefore I can express my problems in a similar way'. Note that this is, in the end, an avoidance of the actual problems he may have. Rather than looking at his problems, finding their shape and dimension and acting in response, the boy uses his friends as an aggressive model to express the difficulties he is only dimly aware of.

Several conclusions follow. First, that aggressive teenage boys often have only a dim awareness of what their difficulties truly are, as these difficulties remain unexamined in the impulse to anger and aggression they have borrowed from their peers or family. They need help to discover not only solutions, but also to understand what their problems are in the first place. Second, the difficulty with unconscious inferences is that they are not as easily open and accessible to discussion and modification as conscious inferences are. Unconscious inferences can be particularly resistant to modification, as the deputy principal found in relation to Alan. In discussing his friendships and the things he gets up to with his friends, a boy might assert (as John implied in his description of the group attack on a boy at school) 'We were just having fun', 'We do things together because I like it', and about questionable characters, 'He's a nice guy, and I like hanging around with him'. The real issue of his membership of such a group in the first place—his half-knowledge of the problems that led to his membership—is seldom acknowledged. This may only be made apparent gradually, and slowly, over time.

Third, what also follows is that groups with large power differences in them do not allow the group to operate therapeutically. Groups with members who have roughly equal power are far more able to produce a quality of 'doing–being' that allows for the extension of self-representation which is fundamental to the successful completion of adolescence. In my group work with boys, I actively listen for the expressions of power within a group and try to assist boys to speak about these power relations. So when one boy raises his fist towards another in order to gain a valued item in a group activity, and the boy with the item noiselessly gives it to him, I ask about this. 'What just happened?' 'Why did Josh give the magazine to John?' I am trying to *turn power relations into communications*. At the start, boys who are menaced by more aggressive boys are often reluctant to answer these questions, so I begin with descriptions of what happened and make guesses.

Over time, as boys realise that anything can be said in the group without fear of consequence, except more saying, these power relations break down as they are spoken about more and more. Equal, or symmetric, social relations result in the development of multiple rational and moral perspectives. Due to this equality of peer relations, not one but multiple perspectives are discussed within the group, resulting in the development of increasingly justifiable forms of rational and moral reasoning: reasoning that is flexible and able to accommodate multiple perspectives. As one of the key 'antidotes to anger' is an ability to reflect on a situation, and allow the sophisticated accommodation of multiple, complex perspectives, membership of the right peer group is crucial to the process of adolescence. Steps for ensuring this are discussed in Part II.

Identification with a violent or aggressive role model or ideal can also be spotted in discussions with boys outside groups. Adolescent boys tend to adopt deviant beliefs as a result of identification with a 'rejected' social group. The influence of rejected peers is very high on the list of negative predictors for delinquency. As rejected peers make friends with other rejected peers who are marginalised at school, an increasing sense of victim-hood prepares fertile ground for anger and anti-social beliefs to develop. Such anti-social beliefs appear most often to be a justification for acting solely in accordance with how an individual feels, as opposed to being prepared to go along with the accepted social order.

In-group identifications can be surprisingly flexible and plastic within a group whereas no amount of persuasion and discussion with people outside the group (for example, parents and teachers) can shift a boy's attachment to a group. Identification with a group is a normal part of adolescence. However, in the case of aggressive boys, it is as if in a group, each finds comfort in numbers: 'You see, none of us are wrong about ourselves. We all share this, therefore we are right about ourselves'. It should be noted, precisely as a result of the identification, that the boys are never clear about what this 'it' is that they share. Identification with such groups deafens the group members to themselves, and a boy can forsake all the years of education and family influence in a breathtakingly short amount of time.

It is important to understand how a boy's peer group functions in this way as it can then be used as a means of modification of some of the most secret inner problems. Boys reveal themselves as they are talking about their activities with their peers, and in their conversations with peers.

Fathers and Alternate Fathers—'Godfathers'

The film *The Godfather*, based on Mario Puzo's book of the same name, is an epic story across three generations of an American–Italian mafia crime family that illustrates many aspects of the changes of adolescence and the influence of the group. Michael, the youngest son of the Godfather, Don Corleone, leaves the family and becomes a war hero in Vietnam. He has two older brothers, Sonny and Fredo. When Michael returns, he is clearly somewhat outside the family, discussing them with his girlfriend as an outsider, as someone who has put his family, and the group of cronies that surround his family, behind him. He reveals to his girlfriend the patriarchal place of his father, 'The Godfather', as the head of the family's crime business and the system of debt, bloodshed and honour that the mafia's system works upon.

When his father is critically injured Michael's older brothers take over running the family's ugly crime business. Sonny, the oldest, has always lived and worked within the business. He is hot-headed, cannot think under pressure and acts in a retributive way about running the family's affairs. 'If they do that to us, then we do that to them' is his way of 'if–then' thinking. His leadership has a paranoid flavour, in that he tends to act counter to his family's interest, blaming people who are innocent and accepting people who are enemies into his inner circle. For example, he orders the killing of a loyal member of the family business following the maiming of his father, even though he simply happened to be with his father at the time. Sonny does not think about where the real responsibility for the murder attempt lies. Sonny meets his doom by walking into a simple trap set by his enemies—one he could have easily avoided by more clear-headed thinking.

Michael's other brother, Fredo, tends to easily fall under the thrall of others' thinking, becoming a slave to them. He is sent to Las Vegas to oversee the family's interests in gambling. There he falls under the spell of a non-member of the family, taking orders from him and following him, betraying his own family's interests.

It is only Michael, who has left the family and been subjected to another form of discipline in the military, another cultural milieu, who can return as his own man, as the one who can think clearly and independently. He is not prone

> to childish fits of anger like his oldest brother, or to being a follower of others like his other brother. Michael's thinking is not paranoid, although he does spend a lot of time thinking about the actions of others. Rather, he shows an ability to understand other people's position and the ways others think. Based on this he draws conclusions, and then acts. Michael can be creative and produce something, which entitles him to the position of Godfather. Despite the ugliness of the crime business the family runs, and despite the fact that Michael's father wished for something else for him, *The Godfather* is an accurate depiction of how a son can come to assume his place through drawing on both the father and other fathers, institutional (that is, the army), cultural and otherwise.

We can contrast Michael's adolescence with that of Douglas in Chapter 3. Douglas was prematurely ejected from his family and spent his teenage years as an outsider, with no family to push against and then return to. He longed for the family he had lost as a child and became trapped within that picture of himself as a child. Michael Corleone's adolescence (and we have to imagine somewhat, as the details of his rite of passage are not given), in contrast, was a clear step away from his family, and involved him in a business that gave him training in a world that separated him from his family. It is the case that both Douglas and Michael stepped away from their families in adolescence, but Michael was able to use his physical absence from the family as a psychical step away. The implications of this are that the manner in which a son steps away from the family is important, and parents should have regard for this.

I am not arguing in favour of military service because the reality of the armed services causes many problems for vulnerable individuals. Rather, I am indicating the importance of a metaphorical rite of passage, which may be impeded or halted by many factors. Below I explore more fully the factors that seem to be crucial in this rite of passage.

Thought, Identity and Morality in Adolescence: Trying It On

Thought

Adolescence is an important period for the development of reflective and critical habits of mind. Adolescents' abilities to think logically and to monitor and reflect on their own and others' cognitive and emotional processes increase dramatically through adolescence. One of the most important of these changes is an increase in rationality, attributable mainly to increases in the ability of adolescents to think about their own thinking. This advance means that adolescents' thinking can become looser and more associative than the 'if–then' thinking of childhood. An example of angry 'if–then' thinking is, 'He hurt me, so I have to hurt him'. It is the sort of thinking prominent when someone is under threat, as was the case with Alan in Chapter 1. An example of a more so-called 'meta-cognitive' mode of thinking, a more thought-through approach, is, 'He's trying to hurt me. This is out of character for him. I wonder why he is doing this'.

An ability to think in the abstract and wonder is not something that just 'switches on' in adolescence: it is influenced by the adolescent's social and family environment. In addition, with the development of reasoning, earlier modes of mental activity are not replaced; rather, they are built upon, and mature individuals still frequently utilise these earlier modes of thought. This is why we observe apparently logical and mathematical thinking in young children (as inference can often appear to be sophisticated reasoning) and fundamental irrationality in adults, who use earlier as well as later modes of thinking.

The Age of Adolescence

In order to understand how thought develops in adolescence, we need to examine briefly the structure of thought. All people use *inference*, which is perhaps the most basic building block of human thought. The structure of inference is given by the if–then structure of 'If he hurt me, then I must hurt him'. Inference involves the generation of a new thought from an old thought. Many emotions are accompanied by such basic inferences, and the 'I'm hurt–hurt him' inference often accompanies anger. It is this type of inferential thinking that Sonny Corleone uses to justify retribution in *The Godfather*. The problem with this type of thinking is that simple retribution may well be against the avenger's best interest.

Thinking may be defined as the deliberate coordination of inferences to serve one's purposes. People think to solve problems, justify actions or claims, or to plan future actions. Though children think, thinking also develops through adolescence, with increases in abilities in problem-solving, decision-making, planning and hypothesis testing.

Reasoning is the constraint of thinking on the basis of a self-imposed standard of rationality. Adolescents generally become increasingly successful at constraining their inferences and thinking to conform to increasingly justifiable norms. In other words, adolescents become increasingly efficient at thinking about and ordering their mental activity in accordance with norms developed in social interactions with peers and family. This results in increases in the ability to perform rational thought.

Instead of thinking and reasoning, aggressive adolescents and men follow a more primitive level of inference that is also characteristic of the group. I once worked with a group of men who were domestic violence offenders. One started to describe an episode in the past of how he had beaten his wife. Though no one in the group had anything much to say about the incident, after the next five minutes the group focused on what the woman had said immediately prior to the violence, and started to agree that if those things had been said to them, well, they would have had no choice but to be violent. The whole group joined this man in agreeing with his 'she provoked me, so I can hit her' thinking. It took the remainder of the group session for the domestic violence offenders to come to other forms of thinking and reasoning that did not entail the aggression-producing 'if–then' mode of thought.

In the case of chronic reactive aggression in adolescents, their norms may be justified by a peer group of other rejected and aggressive peers. Thus the norms of such boys are likely to justify the use of aggression and intimidation that originally (and most likely still do in the case of reactive aggression) served the purpose of defending a fragile sense of self.

Chronic problems with anger often mean such adolescents (and in response their families and friends) utilise automatic, inference-based mental activity prior to their aggressive actions. Reactive aggression is the result of reliance on hostile and other blaming inferences. Not all cognitions are equal: automatic inference is not an act of thinking. Such automatic inferences are likely to be an expression of an underlying fantasy that colours a boy's perception of the world. Containment of anger and aggression may occur as a result of a boy being able to allow thought and reasoning, while resisting the urge to an automatic reduction of tension that results from the use of aggression or violence.

These developing abilities of thought in adolescence can be shaped, and used to question the utility of boys' thinking and beliefs, including automatic judgements, inferences and attributions. This depends, of course, on the proviso that parents and caregivers of adolescents are able to utilise their own abilities in abstract thought to assist with the shaping.

An ability to reflect on the complex and ever-changing field of relationships is crucial here. A paranoid habit of mind means simply allowing an inference—a 'victim view' of the world—to overlay the field of social relations that surround the adolescent. A more sophisticated, critical habit of mind means the boy can constrain his thoughts, based on his aims and a standard of rationality.

At times using one's abilities to allow abstract thought can be difficult, since one of the central battlegrounds between parents and their adolescent son is the field of knowledge. From the parents' point of view, they know best in terms of how to help their son; from the son's point of view he knows best in terms of how to learn for himself. What is important here is not to become entrenched in the battle of who knows best, with the parents taking a position opposite to the son on all matters where his conduct is concerned. The parents would then simply be thinking inferentially and trapping them and the son in a tit-for-tat battle over his behaviour and limits. Understanding that the battle about knowledge is simply part of the developmental trajectory of adolescence places the parent in a different position. Parents can pick their places to make a stand and allow other things to occur, balancing safety against opportunity. I discuss this further in Part II.

Morality

Anyone who has spent time with young children knows that a prohibition creates a wish. Children quickly come to know what is allowed and what is forbidden. In infancy and childhood (and into adulthood), the knowledge that something is forbidden is what creates the wish.

During adolescence, the tendency to view what is forbidden as 'good' continues, but it is also a time where a boy learns to act ethically side by side with his own more socially errant wishes. This involves a difficult, anxious and conflict-provoking journey for both parents and adolescents. As in the beginnings of a critical rationality in adolescence, it is an important moment for the development of a moral compass, a sense of what is right or wrong, in addition to what is the 'good' for the adolescent and what is the 'bad': in short, what they want. There is an overlap between these concerns.

One hopes that during adolescence there is a change from the child-like 'I want it! Give it to me now!', where the boy demands that his environment give him what he wants and if the environment fails him, then anger and aggression result. The change in adolescence to 'I want it, how can I have it?' involves a different approach. Rather than looking to others, or hoping secretly that others might deliver what he wants, the boy learns to act ethically within the normal rules of society towards what he wants. The boy becomes less permeable to his environment and more insistent on his own direction and means of following his own direction.

In the case of Alan there was a relativity in his ethical life, which bent to the demands of the moment. At the moment of persecution, it seemed perfectly justifiable to harm his persecutors. His feeling of needing recompense for the persecution overrode any sense he had of causing harm to others. But when the deputy principal addressed him, however, he gave a convincing performance of regret and sorrow, one that was not simply a performance. Rather it was that Alan had little sense of his internal moral compass and simply bent to the demands of the situation around him.

Morality appears to be made of several aspects. First, it can be said to be a focus on justice and respect for rights: morality is a rational process whereby one can be said to have a greater or lesser developed sense of moral reasoning. A second aspect of morality is a social one, where it can be seen as a matter of care and compassion in the conduct of human relationships. Probably both aspects are important in moral development.

This is where the reasoning aspect of morality becomes important: a boy discovers how a universal law, which may have been repeated to him many times, actually works in practice. Alan could not find a way of reconciling the universal law provided by the principle 'No violence in the schoolyard!' with his own subjective response in the moment of persecution 'I have to get them because what they are saying about me is wrong!' Alan had trouble moving from a universal moral imperative to an individual ethics of action. He received plenty of moral imperatives from teachers, peers and others, but without an ethical framework which could assist him to determine how he acted, the urgings to 'be good' from others amounted to little.

The subjective reality of such ethical principles may only be discovered once boys come close to crossing them, and this commonly occurs in consultation with the ethics of a peer group. Recall the giant hands of the video *Crossing*. Unlike the child and the adult, the adolescent makes these hands permeable and provisional, in order to discover for himself his own understanding of where the law lies.

With his peers, a boy can act in order to discover his subjective renderings of what is right or wrong. The personal reality of morality is seldom found in the enforced morality of institutions (the red light of the pedestrian crossing) or the authoritarian rules of a parent. This is exactly what happened with John when he found his aggression caused him so many problems. As we will see in Part II, eventually he found a means of getting what he wanted in the context of his peer group.

A further aspect of morality is how important moral principles are to a boy. The search for 'Who I am', the adult identity, is strongly influenced by the search for right and wrong, and what is moral or not.

Identity

Identity is the surface expression of the fantasies of the adolescent, fantasies that are an expression of the childhood environment. Identity is a solution to two closely related questions: 'Who am I?'

and 'What do I want?' These questions are adolescent continuations of the child's question to the parent, 'What do you want me to be?' The answer to them in adolescence is often not logical, rational or linear, and may be temporary. In addition, identity presents only a partial answer, taken as it is from the outside.

The term 'identity' comes from the Latin *identicus*, 'to be identical with'. On the one hand, identity is the result of identification—the effort on the child's part to be identical to whomever he identifies with. For the young child this is commonly one or other of his parents. In the normal run of things, the child finds a figure in or close to the family to identify with.

In adolescence, on the core of the experiences the child has within the family, the boy then sets about ordering these experiences with his new-found powers of thought that were discussed above. Within the new ordering, the adolescent undergoes another particularly intense set of identifications with figures outside the family, as a means of finding a pathway out of the family and into his own world. The paradox is that with each new identification, each effort to become identical with someone or something else, the child forsakes what has previously been his. The adolescent forsakes himself all the more he tries to affirm himself within each identification.

Identity appears to be a surface phenomenon, massaged as it is by the mass media's appropriation of culture for commercial purposes. We often find identity expressed in clothes, taste for music, accessories, sports activities, membership of a certain group, and friends chosen. Adolescent beauty and fashion is held up as some sort of ideal of society that adolescents feel that they have to match, live up to, adopt as their own. Thus it is rather unclear what the term 'identity' denotes—is it a transient, fluctuating surface of little significance, or is it of deeper importance, fundamentally determining the future of the adolescent?

The aspect of identity that troubles many parents is a boy's uncritical adoption of values, ideas and friendships that seem inimical to his interests. All of a sudden, a boy starts to act below the level of knowledge, scruples or tact that a parent knows him to be capable of. Despite a parent's or teacher's best efforts to intervene, a boy may insist on doing something inherently silly, misdirected or fruitless. There is a balance to be adopted here, in that such occurrences are potentially problematic for the boy, yet can also be seen as a way of him articulating a difference with his family. To not allow a boy to experiment with his identity, to not allow him some freedom to find his own way, will leave him vulnerable to falling under the sway of others, and will not allow him to develop as a critical and independent thinker.

In brief, we can say that identity is an expression of something taken in by the adolescent from outside, as an unconscious exit strategy from his family. These markers of an adolescent's identity may be discarded, having served their role, once the crisis of separation from the family is over. However, what the adolescent expresses within his identity in an attempt to separate can have very real consequences.

In particular, the type of associates a boy chooses in the articulation of his adolescent identity is important. This is particularly so if he has aggressive or angry tendencies. The most important factor in determining adult outcomes for boys is membership of a group of peers who have little regard for the rule-bound nature of society. The adolescent boy who uses anger and aggression to solve his difficulties and get what he wants in the schoolyard tends to be avoided by his peers, who will be 'on guard' around him. In the schoolyard the boy will tend to be treated in an aggressive manner even by non-aggressive peers. He will find it difficult to make friends and will be rejected. He will fall into a peer group of like-minded others, who have been similarly rejected, and have a vengeful and disgruntled attitude towards the accepted order.

At its worst, the membership of a youth gang under the leadership of a ruthless and powerful member is the ultimate giving up of the self in adolescence. The boy tends to fall under the sway of others, all of whom use an aggressive anti-social stance as armour against the slings and arrows of the world. The boy will be submissive to the group's leader, even when his own best interests are at stake. This is the tragedy of a boy's identification with an aggressive peer group, or youth gang. The boy forsakes himself, his own history and family, for the violent, ruthless ideal of the group's leader.

It is precisely the time where parents must be aware of a boy's associates. As much as possible, a parent's involvement should avoid being authoritarian, imposing an absolute no. Parental involvement will usually work best in a way that allows the son's deviance from his family values to be an opportunity to develop his independence of thought further. The aim of parental involvement is that discussions between parents and sons should not lead to a boy forsaking his family background in adolescence (although there are nearly always aspects of this) but building on the foundations he has been given in the family.

This is closely related to the idea that if a boy emerges from childhood with the broad notion that he has nothing to lose and nothing to protect from his family, then he will act as if he has nothing to lose. The notion of identity, that a boy has a sense of what he wants to be, is protective. By breaking the rules, a boy can lose what he wants to be.

However, if a boy has become deeply involved with peers who are law-breaking and violent, there is a case for parents intervening to remove the influence of these boys.

Adolescent Boys

The difficulties boys have in expressing emotion and the propensity they have to act on their emotions have been well documented.

Throughout their development, boys are commonly not encouraged to speak about their emotions. They often have to rely on action to express emotion, rather than speech. Anger is a method of expressing negative feelings that makes a boy feel powerful and in control, more so than communicating distress by words. Boys tend to feel anger and identify problems in their environment, rather than focus on their inner experience and its meaning in relation to their environment and their actions. In addition, if a boy has become involved in a milieu that condones coercion, he may see little advantage in talking about inner experience. This closing down may be his answer to the difficult question that plagues the adolescent boy as he struggles to make sense of sexual maturity: 'What is a man?'

It presents quite a problem for those parenting and working with angry and aggressive adolescent boys. The closing-off from inner experience found in many angry boys runs counter to the disclosure of thoughts, feelings and responses that is necessary for working through their inter-personal problems. The tendency of boys to act, and then think, must be taken up in discussions with them.

In these dimensions of change in adolescence that I have been covering there is always a trial and error aspect—the young person trying it on to see if it fits. It is the nature of adolescence. The development of adult-like capabilities but with a moratorium on the assumption of adult-like roles allows adolescents the opportunity to try out different aspects of thinking, morality and identity.

All of the so-called 'developments' I have discussed above may give the illusion that there is a natural linear progression from childhood to adolescence to adulthood. However, the onset of sexual function does not cancel or destroy or surpass what happened and the effect of what happened in infancy and childhood. Similarly, an individual's progression to adult roles and responsibilities does not eliminate the marks that the 'rites of adolescence' leave on him. Childhood, puberty and adulthood all leave their traces on the person, in much the same way that an archaeologist uncovers the remnants of previous civilisations as he or she digs through layers of time. The difference with a human being is that any of the stages may hold sway within an individual at any particular time. This is particularly so in adolescence, when at times a pubescent boy seems to retreat to a child-like level but at other times can show remarkable levels of insight and maturity. The fact that these aspects of selfhood coalesce in adolescence presents a major opportunity.

From 'Paranoid' Habit of Mind to 'Critical' Habit of Mind

Angry individuals do not tend to function well inter-personally: they make friends into enemies and are often not the best judges of character, trusting people when there is little evidence on which to base trust. Angry people react to the smallest, unintentional slights, they construe well-meaning advice or comments as being against their interests: this is how they quickly turn friends into enemies. Angry people tend to show a certain knowledge about the world—a 'knowledge' that people are hostile and 'out to get them'. This unspoken reactiveness to others tends to make those who are often in contact with an angry adolescent mimic his pattern of misconstruing innocent actions. We could call it a 'paranoid habit of mind', where everyone and everything is a possible enemy. Aggressive boys appear to have an automatic inference—'People are out to get me, so I'll get them first!' Some children enter adolescence with this view of the world. If adolescence is a time when the way an individual views the world can be fundamentally questioned and reconfigured, then it presents a major opportunity to alter this 'paranoid' world view. It is particularly true given the expanding intellectual and emotional capacities of adolescents. *It is hard to overestimate the centrality of adolescence to forming a 'critical habit of mind', as these intellectual and emotional capacities expand.* A critical habit of mind involves a boy using a self-imposed standard of reasoning to undertake more sophisticated thinking about his social relationships.

Angry individuals have difficulties with critical and rational reflection, particularly given the defensive function of anger. The necessity to defend their aggressive actions may be responsible for shaping the truths that an angry individual holds. Such beliefs also strongly influence the degree to which an individual is prepared to utilise reason or logic. An individual's paranoid knowledge about his or her social world greatly influences his or her reasoning abilities. Paranoid knowledge is knowledge based at the level of automatic inferences of hostility. When things go wrong, angry adolescents tend to act first and think later. As one boy told me once: 'I don't get angry. I just get sore knuckles'.

This calls for intervention from an adult, who can help 'unpack' the action–reaction knot by assisting the adolescent with inserting a pause for reflection between perceiving and reacting. Parents and other adults can travel along with the adolescent, endeavouring to help him build knowledge based on reflection about his ultimately self-destructive aggressive actions, confronting adolescents with evidence of their actions that then becomes the basis of this reasoning process. The reasoning process ultimately aims to question the self-destructive aggressive acts, as questioning may result in a move from the paranoid habit of mind to a critical–reflective habit.

An approach that uses experience, and encourages a boy to reflect on that experience, is therefore superior to adults discussing with the boy right or wrong methods of acting or thinking (that is, trying to get him to identify 'distorted beliefs' or for them to impose morality). This is because discussion of right and wrong is likely to result in an intellectual power struggle, caught in the knowledge–reasoning knot. One encourages the boy to reflect on experience by using an adolescent's own goals and wishes for his life, insofar as he has been able to articulate them. Such an approach fits well with the adolescent pattern of experimentation, reflection and discovery.

Authority, Tolerance and Limits: The Politics of Rules

Adolescence changes the role of the parent in the setting of rules and principles of behaviour. Although a parent can continue to act as they have with their son when he was younger and the parental power was clear, this is not the most advantageous strategy with adolescents. For many adolescents, parents have been deposed from naming matters of the heart to being mere consultants.

Adolescent sons need room to move and thus to allow their cognitive, moral and identity development. As adolescence progresses rules can be seen less as absolute and more as opportunities to allow parents and the son to have discussions (more or less heated) which facilitate the boy's independence. Rules can become a means of making an issue or problem visible, so that it can be discussed. Being too inflexible about rules means that the son may begin to hide his rule-breaking behaviour from his parents, rendering this aspect of the son's life invisible from family.

The teacher, parent or youth worker needs to be savvy and play a game of politics about rules, with the long-term interest of the adolescent in mind. There is a delicate mixing of several dimensions:

- *power*, with at times the adolescent, at other times the parent, acting in a position of power;
- *care*, as it is always the adolescent who needs to be taken care of;
- encouraging *self-responsibility*, by helping an adolescent to develop a critical habit of mind.

In trying to set a general context here, don't allow the details of the argument with your son distract you from the important principle: it is the parent's responsibility to allow the son freedom, but to be firm when a certain boundary is reached. The broader reasons for a boundary being set is something that an adolescent can have difficulty perceiving, despite his protests.

Certainty and Doubt with Angry Adolescents

One of the most difficult problems confronting parents is the 'I know best' attitude of many teenagers, when parents can clearly see that it is not the case. Such certainty can often be an interaction between the 'I'll do it myself' attitude of adolescence along with the doubt-destroying certainty of anger, 'I'm right and no one will tell me otherwise'. It flies in the face of what was discussed earlier, that the certainty of anger hides a doubt—a *profound doubt* about the self.

Perhaps nowhere else are these aspects of the other-blaming tendency in anger more pronounced than in adolescence. The fact that the suffocating (to the adolescent) concerns of the parent are pushed aside can be an important statement of independence on the boy's part. The idealism of adolescence can cause difficulties (not least because it disturbs adults' own lost ideals) when the adolescent finds that the world doesn't fit into his way of viewing things. Anger, being blamed for all sorts of problems, and dismissals of adult knowledge can be seen in the broader context of what is necessary for an adolescent to achieve. Recognising this is to understand that there are other factors at work in an adolescent's irritableness and quickness to anger.

However, it can be quite hard to step back from such confrontations, and the adolescent 'knowing it all' is an important moment. What should parents aim at when discussing and sorting through problems with their son? How can parents respond so as not to denigrate the son's idealism and enthusiasm, but yet foster a degree of realism?

A central skill for parents in such discussions with adolescents is having an ability to resist getting 'it all sorted out'. Whilst there are times where they need to be firm and clear about boundaries, another strategy must also be employed if parents are to encourage the positive changes of adolescence discussed in this chapter. If conversations with an adolescent are beset by vehement certainty on his part, then the method of questioning an adolescent, aiming to create some doubt about his chosen course, may be helpful. The parent's role here, rather than answering questions, is to create questions. Creating questions and expressing doubts in the face of adolescent certainty can be very helpful to the adolescent's development.

Resilience in Adolescence

Rather than being trapped in questions of the past, such as 'What have I done wrong? What has gone wrong?', far more helpful questions parents can ask are focused in the present: 'How can I use the changes of adolescence to help my son?' or 'Are there things that my son does that are helpful and adaptive?'

The answers to such questions may be particularly difficult to find when confronted by the critical, defiant and futile behaviour of many adolescents. Also, the strategies used by adolescents are not predictable. The development of thought, identity and morality discussed in this chapter involves many trials, many errors and self-generated setbacks. What is created in adolescence is often through a method of doing–being (see page 46). Adolescents, by reflecting on their actions, come to a more complex and sophisticated understanding about how relationships, and the social world more generally, works.

We know that young people who do well in later life are those able to learn from the storms of adolescence. This is clear from the way in which resilient adolescents look at and make sense of the world around them. They tend to see nuance rather than generalise about a situation. They can give a coherent, flexible and inclusive account of events, rather than a closed and static one. Such teenagers tend to welcome change as opportunity, and accommodate and tolerate relationships rather than reject others as a threat. But how does one assist an adolescent towards such a means of understanding the world? This is the topic of the following chapters in Part II, where I offer practical steps parents can follow: the Doing Anger Differently program.

In Brief

- Adolescence is a time of intense and profound change. The changes centre on an adolescent acknowledging and questioning what he has previously accepted as fact.
- Adolescents make important advances in thinking and reasoning, moral development and identity. All of these have particular implications for an angry and aggressive boy.
- In the area of *thought*, the move from inference-based thought to reasoning can result in increased abilities of adolescents in thinking about their relationships, reflection and a sense of who or what they wish to be. The relation between possibility and reality is reversed, in that reality was previously a constraining influence. In adolescence, due to new abstractive abilities, reality becomes the basis to extend and enhance their lives.
- The increase in ability to reason means that adolescents can now find and found their own *ethical* standards of behaviour, rather than always relying on parental guides.
- The adoption and 'trying on' of identities contains a danger. The adolescent may be trying on, extending and expanding a sense of being but, on the other hand, he may also be trapping himself in a constrictive, narrow identification with peers whom he perceives as the same as himself.
- As an aggressive boy enters adolescence there is a possibility for him (with the right help) to move from a paranoid, assumption-

driven 'habit of mind' to a responsive, critical and flexible habit of mind.

- Peers have an increasing influence and family a decreasing influence in adolescence, with school forming an important role in mediating between childhood and adulthood.
- The peer group has a significant potential to extend how an adolescent thinks of himself, and it provides a means of differentiation from the family. The peer group also has the potential to limit and confine an adolescent's development if it is an aggressive group that emphasises sameness.

PART II

Doing Anger Differently: Techniques and Principles

This part of the book details a series of broad principles and techniques that adults can use to help an angry boy in a manner that he may accept. The idea is for adults to use aspects of the present to help influence the future of the angry boy. I also outline ways to help the adults stay focused on what they are trying to do, rather than be derailed by the many emotionally draining and distracting problems that are part and parcel of dealing with an adolescent. Techniques give us something to hang on to when we are overwhelmed with emotion ourselves, are confounded or bewildered, or are so exhausted by the conflict we cannot think: many parents have described to me the difficulty of thinking clearly in the heightened, conflicted atmosphere produced by angry adolescents.

Chapter 5 is an overall approach to the myriad issues involved in raising an adolescent, illustrated with a discussion of Ryan's difficulties. It looks at the process of how adolescents gain knowledge, and develops ways to help parents influence and encourage their adolescent son towards creative self-determination. Chapter 6 deals with specific techniques for intervening directly with an angry and aggressive adolescent. Chapter 7 covers broader principles for intervention, and Chapter 8 with intervention in the school context. An Appendix gives information about where further help may be available.

The principles and techniques given here are useful for boys across the spectrum of anger difficulties, from those who have extreme problems such as John's, as well as those who have more mild anger disturbances.

Although Part II can be read alone, Part I provides a deeper and broader context to the techniques outlined here. But before launching into specific techniques, I wish to discuss the outcomes of John's case, which was featured earlier in the book.

John: Beating Victim-hood and Taking Action

John's case illustrates how quite extraordinary changes can occur with adolescents in a short period of time if the right influences and motivations are in place. John's story is a success, despite its grim beginnings in Chapter 1. It illustrates the various techniques I describe later which assist in producing such a change.

> John, who had violently assaulted another boy, came to see me for approximately six months. At the end of this time, he had started to think very differently about his aggression and anger.
>
> John was a big boy, and many boys in his year were scared of him. After two months of sessions with me, he told me that he had been asked to 'sort a guy out' for a friend at school. He said that he had approached the situation cautiously because 'you don't really know what's gone on' and that he wanted to discuss the problem with the boy he had been asked to 'sort out'. This was quite different from the attitude he had adopted in his previous encounters. Rather than assuming that people wanted to attack him, he clearly showed signs of wanting to check things out. He told me that he simply kept his hands in his pockets throughout the whole discussion with the boy, because 'you can't just go in there without knowing what's going on', and that he managed to resolve the conflict between his friend and the other boy without hitting anyone, asking his friend and the boy to 'get along'.

It seems quite a shift for John. He had begun to use words rather than fists to sort out troubles—contrast this with his behaviour in Chapter 1. Though it is true that he was far from being an angel, I emphasised to him the contrast between his restraint in this incident and his previous, violent attack. I did this to try to help John notice—and understand—the meaning behind his actions. It was his changes in behaviour that had led to a better outcome, not chance or external circumstances. Also, he had begun to analyse the social situation, to think about relationships within it, rather than simply overlaying his 'paranoid habit of mind' on his social relations.

John was able to agree with this, but how had this shift started to occur? John had little difficulty in giving clues, which seemed to lie in his changing attitude towards school. John wanted to change his interactions with teachers, but he had begun to feel the weight of his reputation. He was tired of being the one at whom teachers always looked first when there was trouble when their backs were turned to the class, and he hated being accused wrongly. He told me that he really regretted having a heavy reputation that was difficult to throw off. As a result of our reflections, he began to reconsider the value of his relationships, particularly with teachers.

It also seemed that there had been a substantial reordering in John's mind of the importance of his pursuit of enjoyment, what he wanted for his future, and his faith or belief in rules and conventions that govern civil human interaction. In short, it now seemed to him that there was a point to accepting a limit on his pursuit of enjoyment.

Recall John's almost celebratory attitude in the past, as he retold stories of violence towards his peers. John's violence had seemed to rest more on enjoyment of power and dominance inherent in the aggressive act, rather than a reactive, emotional lashing out.

In our meetings, the question that we continually returned to, indirectly, was, 'Why accept a limit on fun and enjoyment?' We did this in a series of discussions that weaved a complex web of meaning around how John viewed his life and relationships. When John told a story about how he had told another boy that the boy was being 'slack' for punching up someone smaller than him, I asked him how this measured against his assault on the fellow student described in Chapter 1. John had to start considering how he had given himself an exception from his own rules, ones that he thought important.

Interestingly, the story of John being asked to 'sort out' someone reveals him in a fatherly position: the one who has the power to decide what is right and wrong, what can and cannot happen—in short, what the rules are. Over the period of our meetings, John shifted from allowing himself an exception from what he thought others should do, to including himself in the rules; he recognised that rules were something that everyone should follow.

He described some of the crazy things his friends did, acting how they pleased, completely outside general rules of society. One had set fire to a dog, another had thrown a chair, breaking the blackboard in class, yet another smoked ten cones of dope each night, and another continually asked girls for sex, calling them sluts if they refused. A phrase that John returned to in describing his admiration for these friends was that 'they just don't care'. We reflected on what the future held for such boys.

John complained that his female maths teacher always picked on him, looking first to him whenever there was any trouble in her class. I asked how things had led to this. John replied that there was a time when he didn't care, and he just did what he wanted in class and in the schoolyard. He described a fantasy that there were tunnels linking all the buildings in the school, allowing one to move, unnoticed, between the administration block, the sports hall, classrooms and the teachers' staff room. This fantasy seemed to represent a dream that John could stay outside of the gaze of school authorities, eluding all of the strictures and requirements that were involved in attending

Doing Anger Differently

school. Over the time of our meetings he seemed to gradually let go of the hold that this fantasy had over his life.

It also seemed that his view of the rules changed somewhat during our sessions. His statement, 'You can't just go in without knowing what's going on', implied a changed stance: John had started to care, had abandoned the 'I don't care' status that placed him outside normal rules and conventions that others followed. John now seemed to act as if there was a law worth keeping, and he included himself within this law. He was limiting the degree to which he could simply act on a whim without any regard for the rules.

After quite a bit of discussion about his reputation, John decided to leave the school he was attending. He changed to one where his uncle had a minor administrative role and that his cousin attended. He told me that he had had long talks with his mother and his uncle about his future, and he had come to several important decisions in consultation with them. He felt his reputation at his original school was so entrenched that he could neither throw it off nor overcome it. However, after several months at the new school he decided he missed his friends too much, and that the original school had suited him better. After more discussions with his mother, he wrote to his original school, asking it to have him back. In the letter he asked the principal for a fresh start, and described how many of his problems had sprung from the fact that he had established a reputation; if the school allowed him to return, he felt that he could do really well. The school agreed to re-enrol him.

I met with John, as is my standard practice, six months after I had finished the original sessions, to see how things were going. He told me he felt much happier and settled now he had returned to his old school. He said that meeting with me had made him realise what a problem his reputation was, but also that he did wish to complete Year 12. He had changed friendship groups: he sometimes ran into his old friends, many of whom were using drugs, and he was shocked that he had once been in their group. He told me, 'I want to go on and make something of myself'.

This was also quite a change. John had exchanged the short-term 'problem solved' rewards from hitting people for the longer term problems that anger and aggression had created for him. He had done this primarily, in my view, because he had realised that he wanted to make something of his life. He realised he had something to lose.

John's act of leaving his original school and then asking if he could return showed a degree of concern for his future—he was articulating that there was something he wanted to be. This is not the act of someone outcast and marginalised from the mainstream, but of someone attempting to take his future into his own hands. John had moved into being a member of his community rather than acting as a child, demanding to do as he pleased. He had become a truly active participant in his life: rather than being tossed on the sea of his reactions to others, he had decided something needed to be done to renegotiate his relationships.

Many of the important changes that John made were after discussions with his family. His case shows how the involvement of family members is necessary, even when an adolescent is acting in a manner as extreme as John had been doing. Talking with his mother helped him realise that he was able to take charge of his life. She helped him comprehend what he needed to do to gain what he wanted. John's story illustrates how it is possible for parents and teachers to help a boy return from a place that seems quite outside the reach of anyone who might assist.

5
The Cycle of Identity: Reaction, Reflection, Action

Part I of this book demonstrated that in the case of an angry adolescent, the trajectory of adolescence is especially difficult, as a boy may be continually taking a defensive stance of 'I am not wrong about myself'. There are many situations in the schoolyard, in the principal's office, in the psychiatrist's rooms, where a boy has to close off certain parts of himself and return to this defensive stance, vulnerable as he is to attacks. His angry stance against the world often means that he refuses to admit that there is a problem.

The boy's anger is a symptom of the way he views his social world and his place within it—in short, the sort of meanings he arrives at. The degree to which he is flexible in his approach to problems—the more he is specific rather than vague when he analyses social situations, the more he understands the complexity of social interactions, and is able to tolerate the ambiguity involved in most social encounters—the more he is able to skilfully adapt to and learn from his social world.

It is precisely the ambiguity and complexity of social encounters, and the doubt these create, which can produce anxiety in adolescents, an anxiety that 'the certainty of aggression' seeks to put an end to. To help angry adolescent boys one must find a way to allow them to make sense of and embrace social complexity.

This chapter focuses on how parents and carers of adolescent boys can encourage the boys *to listen to themselves*. Adults can promote the way boys develop an understanding of social complexity—develop 'meaning-making' abilities—by taking up certain positions in discussions, positions which will change depending on the difficulties with which the adolescent is struggling. Generally, adults will be aiming through discussions to help a boy shift from the idea of 'I am not wrong about myself' until he is able to examine and listen to his inner 'myself'.

'Doing–Being' and the Acquisition of Knowledge in Adolescence

The toddler, as she tires, may pick up a doll, cover it with a blanket, cuddle the doll and rock it from side to side, put it down, rewrap the doll in the blanket and so on. Toddlers, for the most part, play, or do, how they feel. Adults, on the other hand, will say, 'I'm tired and I'm going to bed'. Adults tend to express their inner state in words.

Most adolescents are still caught between the child's medium of play as a means of self-expression and the adult's cognitive manipulation of ideas and their expression in speech. Adolescents may swing between playing out, or acting out, their ideas at one moment and at other times express them in speech directly and clearly. Most commonly, though, adolescents tend to mix these two modes of expression: using experiencing and acting to understand themselves. I call this 'doing–being', and it is behaviour that is particularly prominent in groups. Adolescents use their actions to then understand their inner state and the world around them. After acting, the thinking and speaking tend to occur. This is one of the primary modes of acquiring knowledge in adolescence: experimenting through action and then reflecting on it with newly found thinking and reasoning abilities. (It is also characteristic of adulthood, but the acquisition of knowledge can be particularly intense during the

The Cycle of Identity

search for adolescent identity.) So in adolescence an action–reflection mode of acquiring knowledge seems to predominate, made possible by new and expanding abilities in thought, and resulting in a sense of discovery and readiness to experiment.

Talking about emotional issues in a purely adult way can cause difficulties for adolescents. In Chapter 3 I gave an example of boys discussing a difficult topic—grief and the loss of maternal figures—but such a detailed elaboration on difficult themes is rare among adolescents. In the case of that group it caused distress, which the boys expressed in various forms of disruptiveness in the following weeks during group meetings. The boys were unable to use only speech to express their difficulties; they also had to act. I am not maintaining that the discussion about loss was damaging, but just that it had consequences. It was my job as an adult to 'read' these consequences and reveal them to the group, so the boys could continue the struggle to express emotional difficulties in speech.

I outline in this chapter a way of communicating with adolescents, discussing ideas and issues, that takes account of the process of 'doing–being'. Essentially, it involves utilising the adolescent sense-making process, 'doing–being', to move the boy from a paranoid to a critical way of thinking.

Being the Parent of an Adolescent

There has been much discussion so far of the tension inherent in being a parent to an adolescent. On the one hand, parents should allow an adolescent to 'find his own way', letting his mental and emotional management abilities develop through adolescence. On the other hand, how do parents remain involved with their son, particularly if they are witnessing some worrying developments?

The parent should attempt to follow a path of 'intellectual midwifery', drawing out wisdom and meaning inherent in, or implied by the adolescent's words. I do not mean that adults should point out all of a boy's mistakes and errors of thinking, with the parent engaging in a mental joust with their son. Another way to describe this position is one of 'emotions coach', where the parent can help a boy struggle with his volatile and reactive inner life by gently prompting him to 'put it into words'. The parent aims to 'ride along' with the boy's pronouncements, in order to help him develop his own stance within the world. This is not the only stance a parent should take with his or her son: there are moments which call for other positions. It is a matter for parental judgement as to how and when to act as intellectual midwife.

Three 'Antidotes to Anger'

To act as an intellectual midwife could be taken to mean that if parents are endlessly curious about their son's ramblings it will result in some change in him, but this is not the case. Parents must be more focused than this. There are three aspects of mental functioning that adults can attempt to draw out of an adolescent:

- a focus on relationships;
- a capacity for reflection and sense-making;
- a sense of how to protect his ability to act.

These three areas are interdependent, and are often deficient in chronically angry boys. I'll discuss each in turn.

An adult's aim should be to attempt to help an angry and aggressive adolescent increase his capacities in each of these areas. Increases in such capacities are expected as adolescence develops but angry and aggressive boys seem to be deficient in them. Attempting to increase these capacities is not easy: it is a complex and cooperative task, which involves attention to the individual difficulties of an adolescent.

Focus on Relationships

In the earlier examples of Alan and John, we saw that they focused on short-term gains that come from an aggressive act—the release of tension and feeling of victory that results. The longer term impact of acting in such a way can be described almost entirely as the result the aggression has on a boy's relationships. A key factor that determines the degree to which a boy emerges from adolescence with the potential for a happy and successful life is the degree of his sophistication in thinking about and acting within relationships. The level of sophistication can generally be judged by:

- how much a boy values, and invests in, his relationships;
- to what degree he is prepared to work hard by reflecting on his position within these relationships;
- how much energy he is prepared to spend cultivating them.

The essence of a boy's reflection on relationships should be *inclusive of himself*, rather than a paranoid exclusion of himself from his own critical thinking.

Capacity for Reflection

By 'capacity for reflection', I mean an ability to think separately from one's own immediate needs and being able to listen and understand one's own and others' points of view. Most centrally, I am concerned with a boy's ability to have his 'I' listen to his 'myself', something that was difficult, for example, for Alan to do (see page 13). Listening to oneself means being able to put oneself in the picture, asking the questions 'Where am I in all of this?', 'How have I been implicated in what has happened?' Needless to say, improving a boy's abilities to reflect improves how he handles his relationships, as well as his capacity to take control of what he does, to act meaningfully in the world.

To improve the capacity for reflection, speech is the key. Speaking is such a straightforward, everyday activity, but if a *reflective kind of speech* can be encouraged between an adult and an adolescent, it can aid enormously in the boy's process of reflection, and increasing his capacity to reflect. Over time, an adolescent gets better at listening to his own speech—either uttered through his mouth, or the internal talk that goes on in his head.

Anger is antithetical to such critical reflection. Anger involves a continual blame of others, and inability to see how one is placed in the whole picture. It is perhaps the capacity for critical reflection that Ryan, in the example on next page, lacks most, thus hampering his relations with others (particularly teachers) and putting obstacles in the path of his desired future.

Sense of Ability to Act

Being *able to act* implies one has a belief that what one does and says are important, and are directed towards some aim. Those who hold this belief tend to be protective of their ability to act on their own behalf, always looking to increase their opportunities for independent action. The direction towards an aim relies on reflection. Angry boys typically react to what is external, rather than act for their own benefit; they have little aim in mind apart from their immediate surroundings.

I discussed in Chapter 1 how boys with chronic anger commonly view the world in two recurrent ways. First, they blame others when things go wrong. Second, they believe good things that happen are caused by others or random events around them. *They have little sense of their own ability to act, and to influence or change the world around them.* They also tend to view their relationships as problematic or threatening, and have little sense of how to use relationships in a way to achieve their own wishes. Below is the story of Ryan, who was fiercely protective of his wish to 'do it myself' and hated teachers taking this away from him; he had little capacity to reflect on how best to protect his ability to act.

The Cycle of Identity

> Ryan was a 13-year-old boy whom I met with for one term at his school. He was often given detention, was disliked by his teachers and was frequently sent to the principal's office after getting into arguments with teachers and subsequent disobedience.
>
> Ryan told me that he particularly disliked his woodwork teacher, Mr Johnson. Ryan hated the way Mr Johnson was always 'the boss' and wouldn't let him do things on his own in the woodwork room. Mr Johnson had told Ryan that 'he couldn't be trusted'.
>
> From Ryan's viewpoint he was both mistrusted by this teacher and also given insufficient guidance to complete tasks successfully. 'He tells you to do something, like make a stool, but he doesn't tell you how to do it. Then he just pushes you out of the way when you're trying to figure out the best way to do it.' Ryan could not articulate the problem of the lack of guidance from the teacher in a way that he could make use of. Even though he liked woodwork, he would often be unable to contain his anger and would argue with Mr Johnson, swearing at him, and thus found himself at the principal's office regularly during woodwork.

Ryan and I had a series of meetings over three months and the results were positive. Teachers told me that Ryan's behaviour in class improved greatly, although Ryan couldn't see what all the fuss was about. This improvement was demonstrated very dramatically when I met Ryan for a follow-up session six months after we had finished the original course of meetings. I had left the door to my room ajar and the deputy principal had seen Ryan with me; he came into the room and said, 'Ryan, I'm proud of you. You have done very well. I haven't seen you at all for the last six months, and that's great. I've been hearing from teachers that you have been getting on and doing your work and not causing too many problems, so well done. Keep up the good work.'

The deputy principal was able to congratulate Ryan for something that was not usually recognised in the normal running of the school. He was able to put Ryan's achievement into words for the boy. This is an important point for parents who are caught up in daily conflict with their son: the conflict should not prevent (although it often does) parents from being able to recognise positive aspects of a boy's behaviour, no matter how small.

What were the clues to Ryan's success? Simply, the success had been a result of discussion between us on three levels—perception, meaning and performing—and for me to respond in myriad ways on each of these levels, according to the topics that Ryan talked about each week. I'll unravel the clues to Ryan's success in the pages that follow.

The 'Cycle of Identity' in Adolescence

The problem of how parents—and other adults who work with adolescents—can involve boys in meaningful discussions about events in their lives has been mentioned several times so far. If there are many conflict-filled and aggressive incidents both within and outside the family, these may be difficult to talk about, both because of a boy's defensiveness about them and the parents' concern that their boy should get the 'right message'. It often means there is no room left for fostering the son's developing independence.

I have also outlined how the way adolescents make sense of their world—what I call 'meaning-making'—determines how well they will deal with it. There are at least three levels involved in 'meaning-making':

1. The *perception* of events; in other words, the manner in which a boy perceives action in the world, and describes the action in language.

2. The *meaning-making* involved in making sense of these events.

The Cycle of Identity

3. The *performing* of this meaning, based on the understanding the boy has.

In the case of angry and aggressive boys, intervention by adults is an attempt to transform these aspects, from automatic aggression into a situation where a boy has a choice as to how he may respond. This represents the move from a 'paranoid' to a 'critical' habit of mind.

Whether the boy is able to discuss an event at a level of perception, meaning-making or performing determines the response of the adult. I'll explain each in turn.

Perception: From Action to Description

Starting with the problem of how Ryan viewed his situation, I asked Ryan how he knew that Mr Johnson hated him. He replied that Mr Johnson always bossed him and did things on Ryan's woodwork projects that Ryan himself wanted to do. I replied that it seemed he didn't like teachers who wouldn't let him 'do his own thing' and discover by experimentation. Ryan agreed. Early in our meetings, I wondered, without expecting an answer, 'What is Mr Johnson doing when he pushes you out of the way?' Ryan then related an incident where another boy had hurt himself by 'doing his own thing'. Was Mr Johnson being careful in taking over some tasks from Ryan?

This conversation continued over a few sessions, examining Ryan's assertion that Mr Johnson hated him. It seemed that the relationship between Ryan and Mr Johnson had grown from a mild, unspoken disagreement into something much bigger, both from the boy's perspective and the teacher's side. Ryan didn't appear to have the means to find his way out of the mutual hostility, and he was getting a bad reputation by continually falling into the trap of the hostility. I made a mental note to work on helping Ryan to use words to make requests to Mr Johnson: it would be preferable to a silence both sides took to be angry or hostile.

Absences, inaccuracies and biases exist within everyone's perceptions of their social interactions, both in regard to their own actions and those of others. Strictly speaking, these biases are how a person 'sees the world'. As such the biases are not distortions of reality or incorrect ways of viewing the world. Rather, they make up part of the substance of who an individual is, and how he or she habitually makes sense of the world. Gaining knowledge about these biases can really only happen through listening to a young person talk about his or her experience. It seemed that part of Ryan's make up, in absence of other evidence, was to assume that a teacher disliked him.

When a parent or adult hears such biases, the natural reaction is to correct the youngster, to inform him how the world 'really' functions. The immediate reaction to listening to Ryan's complaint might be: 'No, it can't be true that Mr Johnson hates you!'. Such an urge to impart a 'correct view' should be resisted, as by intervening too early the adult loses the opportunity to gain knowledge of what the young person is actually saying. Acting quickly when one hears an adolescent articulate a view of the world that one does not agree with, is to impose an understanding on the boy. An adult's view of the world is something which a child laps up, hungrily devouring a point of view and stance about the world, but in adolescence the situation is different.

Recall John's description of the violence he and his friends committed on a classmate. John either glossed over many aspects of the scene as he described it, or described it in a particular way. So I probed further. Why were John and his friends sick of this boy? What had he done to provoke the attack? How was this attack allowed to go on? What was the nature of the boy's injuries? How long did he have to spend in hospital? How did the boy react to the attack? Could John see the boy's face when he hit him with his ring? If so, what did John see?

The Cycle of Identity

During the group, John's discomfort grew as I started to ask him these questions. They presented aspects of the incident to him that he had left out in the retelling, as he attempted to continue his enjoyment of the event and to promote a certain image of himself to his friends. What had been left out of the story were aspects that deviated from principles that were important to him, such as 'You can't hit someone weaker than yourself'. My questions led him to measure his actions against his ethics and this, in turn, led to him declaring later in the group, 'You can't just jump into a situation without knowing what's going on'.

I wish to expand on several important aspects of this movement from action to description. The most important part of talking with a boy like John about an aggressive act is helping him *put the act into words*. This statement might seem ridiculous, like saying the good thing about talking is talking. What I am saying here is that speech itself has effects. Often, in the impulsive acting on anger, the act resulting from anger has eluded speech. Remember that the child's mode of playing out his or her experience still retains a strong hold in adolescence. Speaking removes an act from the realm of a purely physical reaction to emotion, and gives structure and form to the experience. The process of speaking about an event makes the event an object of reflection. Over time, simply speaking about experiences in this manner (and often speaking about the difficult parts of experience such as aggression) can loosen the tie between feeling and acting.

How does one start on such a task? Attempt to lay bare the absences, inaccuracies and biases in perception as a boy talks. Push him gently to fill in the gaps and overcome the normal restraints of his descriptions. Encouraging boys to engage in more detailed descriptions of conflict situations can elicit what is hidden or absent in the account for various reasons. Speaking in such a way can also begin to help the young person take account of other, alternative descriptions or understandings of the event. Such an alternative was beginning to be formulated when John became uncomfortable about the questions I asked him in the group. These are the beginnings of new ideas, for which the adult acts as a midwife. These other meanings are in contrast to the automatic meanings that angry and aggressive individuals tend to overlay on their social perception.

Adults should not to try to impose a 'true description' of the event on the adolescent. Rather, the aim is to open participants to possibilities. To attempt to impose meaning risks arousing the same oppositional tendencies that caused the problem in the first place, and runs counter to encouraging the social development of adolescents.

When eliciting descriptions of events from boys, the following principles apply:

- The way an individual views the world is an unconscious expression of who or what he is.

- Putting the act of aggression into words is productive as it gives structure and form to the experience, which can loosen the automatic link between feeling and acting.

- Speaking about angry reactions can mean that speech may intervene between the feeling and the action of aggression (be it verbal or physical) in the future.

- Speech does this by imposing a form on the feeling, which creates an object for reflection.

- In discussion, seek for what is hidden and absent; be the midwife of new ideas, rather than the boxer pounding an opponent into submission.

- Help the boy make sense of his volatile emotions by coaching him to speak about his feelings. Don't tell him his anger is 'wrong'.

The Cycle of Identity

- Be curious while keeping to broad brushstrokes. Choose your target in each conversation, rather than trying to achieve everything in one encounter. Bogging a boy down in details may frustrate him, so keep to a key point per discussion.

- Don't attempt to impose a 'true' or 'morally correct' description on the boy.

- In certain instances it is fine to express your own viewpoint, but be clear that it is your viewpoint and you are not forcing the boy to take up your view.

- Don't threaten or try to enforce authority over the boy. Adolescents, for the most part, are honest and productive when they feel that the relations of power are equal. This is why the right type of adolescent peer group is so important.

- If you are in a position of authority over a boy, be clear about any 'No' that you have to enforce. Being clear in this way can mean further discussion, which can allow the reasons for his actions to emerge.

Meaning-making: From Description to Constructing Meaning
Lots of ideas had leapt into my mind as Ryan began to talk a little with me about his problems with teachers. Though his worst problems were with Mr Johnson, he had difficulties with others as well. Did Ryan just cause trouble to 'get attention'? Unlike other boys in his classes, who seemed to cope just fine, did he need to make a fuss when he wasn't at the centre of things? Or was he simply just enjoying making a fuss? I tried to put these rather attractive but clichéd hypotheses aside and asked Ryan about what his understanding was.

He told me he didn't like being angry—but then why, I thought, was he causing all of these problems with teachers? In fact he told me that it 'sucked' being so angry all the time and he would do anything to try to stop it. I asked if this meant that we could cooperate to do something about the problem of his anger. He agreed. This was an important step: Ryan had moved from the 'it's everyone else's fault' to agreeing that he wanted to do something about the problem.

Over time, we discussed his love of woodwork, how he had stopped enjoying it this year, and he wanted to start enjoying it again. We also examined his claim that Mr Johnson was being a boss. After discussing this, it became clear to Ryan that he was not learning from Mr Johnson when Ryan was angry with him because he felt he was being pushed out of the way. We discussed the possibility of Ryan learning from Mr Johnson: that he was not being pushed away, but that Mr Johnson was showing him something.

It unfolded that Ryan's aim was to learn as much as he could from woodwork because he wanted to work as a carpenter or builder. We talked about whether being angry with Mr Johnson was helping, and Ryan agreed that it wasn't. This was important, because it gave Ryan a reason to not necessarily act on his anger, as he had a greater goal: to learn as much as he could about woodwork, despite his difficulties with the teacher.

In these discussions we basically examined the meanings Ryan had placed on the situation, and discussed other possible meanings. I had to put aside my ideas about Ryan's actions in order to help him discover his meanings.

This is the second dimension by which adolescents make sense of their world: by *meaning-making* on the events they see and describe. Meaning-making is something that occurs in and about relationships, within the family, with friends and within the school and clubs a boy belongs to. These relationships serve as the stuff, or material, for discussion in this level of 'meaning-making'. The meaning Ryan had made of his relation with Mr Johnson was that Mr Johnson hated him.

However, a key assumption here is that events have more than one meaning, and the meanings a boy imposes on social events that happen around him are strongly influenced by his peers, the

The Cycle of Identity

institutions he participates in and his family, although the family holds less and less influence as adolescence proceeds. Nevertheless, *parents and adults in contact with the boy are in a key position to discuss and shape the meanings he places on events as these meanings emerge.* In my discussions with Ryan it became possible that Mr Johnson was at least in part doing his job as a teacher and it was also possible for Ryan to learn from him.

The meanings that we are most interested in are those that influence how the boy looks at his relationships. Once descriptions of actions have been elicited, the meanings that are assigned to them may then emerge. There is often a back and forth between description and meaning in discussions about anger and aggression. The meaning assigned to aggression within the moment of its expression tends to be automatic and hostile. The aim is to bring about a more reflective consideration of the nature of aggression.

Rather than overlaying a paranoid habit of mind ('He's pushed me out of the way, so I'm going to have to get him back in some way'), Ryan came to think about his relationship with Mr Johnson in a way that he could use to his own advantage. Over time, a boy may be in a position—once they have engaged in an ongoing dialogue with someone about the reasons for their anger and aggression—to make sense of what was previously outside the realm of speech. This in turn may result in a re-evaluation of the meanings a boy has already attributed to his aggression, or to his reason for aggression. As it was reported that Ryan's relations with other teachers also changed for the better, it seemed he was able to use his understandings with Mr Johnson in his classes with other teachers.

This all sounds very nice, but in practice, what does it mean parents and adults should say to or discuss with a boy? The following points may help:

- **Be on the look out for the 'It's not fair!' of anger.** Try to help the boy to say exactly what it was about the situation that was unfair.

Doing Anger Differently

- At times adults may need to make a guess about the emotion or thought underlying the aggressive action. This 'reading' of a boy's behaviour should always be made tentatively, as a way of inviting the boy to comment on his possible motivations.

- Acknowledge the kernel of truth in any perception of unfairness, however out of proportion it seems to the boy's resulting act of aggression or retribution.

- Acknowledging the boy's perception of unfairness may need to occur repeatedly if a relationship of trust does not exist between the boy and the adult. A boy has to know that an adult understands or acknowledges his point of view.

- Help a boy to identify the positive and negative consequences of his actions. For instance, 'Yes, Caleb hasn't teased you since you hit him' balanced against 'What do your friends think about what you did?'

- Bring out the conflict around the aggressive act, without telling a boy what to do. For example, you could say, 'It seems like the problem is solved for now, but I wonder how many friends you are going to have if you hit them when they annoy you, like you hit Caleb?'

- There will need to be a point where one stops 'playing along' with a boy's perception of unfairness, usually by highlighting to him how his aggression created his own doom. Limiting a boy's perception of unfairness will allow his own goals and wishes to enter the discussion.

- Be an 'emotions coach' by highlighting the disturbances caused by feelings that seem to disappear at more rational moments.

- Don't let a boy quash the problem that his anger raised by saying, 'What I did was wrong and I won't do it again' or similar. Accept

The Cycle of Identity

his good intentions, but continue to keep the problem of his anger alive. You could respond, 'OK, but what about how angry you got? What are you going to do with your anger next time if you don't hit someone?'

- Distrust simple or glib solutions put forward by the boy, while accepting the good intention: 'OK, walking away is not a bad idea, but there's still a problem, because this anger will still be eating away at you'.

In the search for meaning between adolescent and adult it is important to hold in mind previous conversations and ideas the boy has discussed, and build on the meanings that the boy has adopted in the past.

Meanings that commonly accompany reactive aggression often exclude the possibility of other, non-violent, means of action. Several areas are of particular interest.

Vulnerability and victim-hood

As we have seen, angry and violent boys tend to endorse their own and others' aggressive acts as well as perceive themselves as victims. This may seem contradictory, even nonsensical to a parent. However, it is often this sense of victim-hood that fuels aggressive acts. The vulnerability of an aggressive boy must be searched for and acknowledged. In order to help an angry boy, it is necessary to 'get inside' their processes of meaning-making, and this inevitably includes looking at the 'It's not fair' of the angry boy.

Short-term gains over long-term gains

Boys typically select short-term gains as a justification for their actions. These include the feeling of being a victor, the image of themselves it promotes amongst their friends, and the reduction in internal tension that follows an aggressive act: problem solved. This was somewhat the case for Ryan: his swearing at Mr Johnson solved the problem of the tension created by his perception of being 'bossed around'. However, many boys fail to recognise the link between their aggression and the problem of their reputation within school and amongst their peers. Ryan had not realised how much his problem with Mr Johnson had got in the way of learning something he loved.

The problem of reputation and relationships
Following a discussion of the 'It's not fair' of anger—that is, the 'Why did you do this?'—the short-term gratification that follows from impulsive aggression can be weighed with the boy against the long-term problems that his aggressive identity causes in his interactions with family, peers and school. These long-term consequences are apparent within a boy's relationships and his construction of them.

A boy's view of his social world is strongly linked with his propensity to anger: changes in reactive aggression usually involve a boy examining and changing his understandings about these relationships. It may not be apparent to the boy that how he has acted in the past contributes to the nature of these relationships. In particular, his sense of victim-hood should be related to his actions. A boy's sense of himself as a victim is variously apparent in his descriptions of his 'reputation', his relation with a particularly 'hated' teacher, peer or sibling, or perhaps a sense that he may have no friends or peers with whom he has a relationship of trust—often precisely because of his reputation.

Discussion can centre on these relationships, which are very important to the process of adolescent development. Adults should work towards unveiling to the boy the difference between the picture he has of himself and the one that he presents to others through his aggressive actions. Once a boy has become aware of how he appears to others, he may be in a better position to change this representation. A boy may then find himself in the position of having

The Cycle of Identity

to teach the teacher, or re-educate his friends and acquaintances about who he is.

A second opportunity for discussion is a boy's ethical beliefs. Angry individuals often have a keen sense of justice—and injustice. Adolescence is an important time for ethical development and there are many opportunities to debate the rights and wrongs of various acts with an angry and aggressive boy. Again, the emphasis here is not to impose one meaning, but to encourage the expression of multiple viewpoints in the group, family or gathering. Thus it is important that a boy be exposed to other individuals, father figures and contexts, so that he can explore and test multiple ideas and principles, as a means of encouraging his ethical development.

In addition, the difference between a boy's view of the meaning of his aggressive action and someone else's view of these same actions is important. Recognising there is a difference opens a boy to the consideration of other possible meanings, and raises questions about the usefulness and ethics of aggression. (Discussion could include questions such as 'What would your father/grandfather/Uncle Joe say about that?') This is in contrast to the anti-social norming common in groups of aggressive boys. Such in-group views—which endorse aggression—hide doubt, create certainty and assuage negative self-feelings but do not result in a boy questioning his pattern of social relations.

In summary, discussing a problem in this way, may, over time, have an effect on the boy. He may decide there are aspects of his actions that were justified, and others that were not. Ryan was able to constrain his thinking to an increasingly justifiable standard. What were the criteria for this justification? The answer should be clear by now. A series of questions revealed Ryan's position to himself: 'What part do I play in this?', 'What do I want?', 'What do I need to do to get it?'. This form of reasoning, which is not always logical, can be expressed in a shorthand way as: *listening to oneself in the context of one's own relations*. This is much better than the automatic overlay of 'It's unfair', through which angry boys tend to view their relations.

It is important to look for moments where a boy moves to a more considered response, and to enlarge or emphasise this shift. It may also be that violence ceases to become the only response to the experience of anger. Essentially, the nature of a boy's response can become more of a choice.

We can contrast this way of speaking with Alan's automatic adoption of the deputy principal's demands that he conform to the school rules. This is an imposition—indeed, a necessary imposition from the school—but it did not solve the problem of Alan's anger.

Performing-meaning: From Constructing Meaning to Action

How can parents see the positives in their boy's behaviour given all the difficulties he presents, diagnoses he may collect and negative influences he seems to wish to absorb? In the darkness of a stormy, angry adolescence, how can parents see the signs of healthy behaviour, of the movement towards self-determination that adolescence is supposed to be all about? In short, how can parents recognise their son's achievements? And how can they reward them, beyond a simple 'Well done' or pat on the back—which can ring a little hollow if it occurs in the context of ongoing conflict?

If a positive act appears to come from nowhere, there is a tendency for an adult to congratulate a boy on his achievement without tying the achievement to the boy's actions or endeavours. The results will be disappointing, as a boy will fail to understand the means by which he acted. The adult must help the boy recognise the active part he played in a positive outcome. How did the act come about? What did the boy do differently to other occasions that allowed him to perform the act?

Recognising positives does rest on the other two steps of the cycle that I have just outlined, description and constructing meaning from

The Cycle of Identity

that description. Careful attention to the dance between description and meaning that a boy assigns to his world will have effects in his actions. It is often *up to others* to help a boy recognise his own achievement. In this recognition, discussion at the level of description and meaning are necessary, prior to the young person being able to make sense of his achievement and the recognition that parents, teachers or coaches are giving them. *This is why simply 'focusing on the positives' fails to help a boy change his aggressive actions.* Just as adults need to help an adolescent by 'reading' his aggressive and destructive acts ('making-meaning'), so too a boy's positive acts need attention. There are several reasons for this.

Angry adolescents easily attribute 'the problem' as something to do with another person, and that this other person should solve the problem. This tendency also crosses over into positive acts and solutions: *angry boys think things go well because of other people*. Angry boys commonly have little sense of how they have acted differently to bring about a positive outcome.

In Ryan's case, after we had talked quite a lot about the goings on in the woodwork room, he casually let it be known one session that he hadn't been sent out of woodwork that day. This was rather unusual. I asked him what he thought of this, and he shrugged. 'Mr Johnson was probably in a good mood.' When I questioned him further, he described a fairly typical lesson: Mr Johnson had stepped in and completed a task on the drop saw without allowing Ryan to see or understand what he was doing. I knew quite well, from numerous previous discussions, that at such a point Ryan would usually swear at Mr Johnson and be sent to the deputy principal.

When I asked Ryan what he in fact had done, he told me that he just stepped back and said nothing. When pressed, Ryan told me that he was angry, but he didn't see the point in telling Mr Johnson about it. He decided to step back and watch what Mr Johnson was doing. This event could be described as an 'exceptional outcome'. It was exceptional in that nothing could have predicted that Ryan was going to respond in this way. It was an outcome in that Ryan did not act destructively and did not have to be sent to the deputy principal yet again. I had to emphasise both of these points to Ryan in order for him to half-heartedly agree that the outcome was in fact something different.

A boy stepping back from a confrontation may not seem to be exceptional at all. To a casual observer, Mr Johnson, the deputy principal and even Ryan's close friends, the act of stepping back would probably pass unnoticed. However, to paraphrase the first moon explorer, it was a giant step back for Ryan, given his history with teachers in general and Mr Johnson in particular. Ryan's act was, in the end, one of containment of his own internal tension. I was able to notice the exceptionality of Ryan's step backwards because I had been engaging him in many discussions about his difficulties. In the normal course of things, however, Ryan's act would have sunk into the uniform grey of his life without him having gained anything from this feat.

The greatest recognition was to come later, from someone Ryan actually had a lot to do with in his life, the deputy principal. The recognition was the result of many later small acts of containment that Ryan managed, which became easier and easier the more he acted in this way. It should also be pointed out that Ryan was lucky to have been noticed in this way by the deputy principal, probably due in part to my presence.

Largely, in the case of Ryan, no one noticed that he had stepped back from confrontation because his act was one of emotional containment. He was angry and he withstood the tension of his anger in order to not do something, although this 'not doing' was both different and difficult for him. But no one else in the room

The Cycle of Identity

would have been able to notice what he was doing, as there was no external sign of how difficult it was. Many boys have talked with me about their attempts over many weeks to 'be good' and complained of their disappointment when no one in their lives, parents or teachers, notices their efforts. It is one of the difficulties angry and aggressive boys face: there are few ways in which they are recognised for withstanding their impulse to act aggressively. This is why it is important to establish with the boy his own reasons for containing his anger and aggression. What does he stand to gain? For Ryan it was his love of woodwork and his access to learning this craft. In the approach I advocate, it is important to understand how a boy thinks and reacts, so that similar events—'being good'—can be recognised. Sometimes this can be a parent's role, sometimes a teacher's, and at other times, as was the case with Ryan, a therapist's.

Adolescents seldom announce their achievements as, 'Guess what? I did really well today!' Adolescents do not tend to claim to understand something as important, or have moments of insight, in the same manner as adults. Rather, teenage boys often bring answers to their dilemmas through recitations of their experiences. Teenagers tend to act on their insights, and their understandings may be made apparent in the form of actions. Adults often only come to know about adolescents' insights through adolescents describing their actions. This means adults have to ask, and that it is up to the adult to help the adolescent understand the exceptionality of their act. I cannot say too often that this 'exceptionalness' can be recognised only if an adult knows a boy well, and has had previous discussions with him about the challenges that face him.

With Ryan, I had returned to helping him describe his acts again—helping him understand he had done something as a result of his discussions and the meaning-making he had carried out with me.

This is what I call 'performing-meaning'. It forms part of a cycle that moves from action to description to meaning and back to action. This cycle, which can be held in mind to assist in structuring discussions with adolescents, can be depicted in the following diagram.

```
              ACTION
            PERFORMING


   MEANING              DESCRIPTION
```

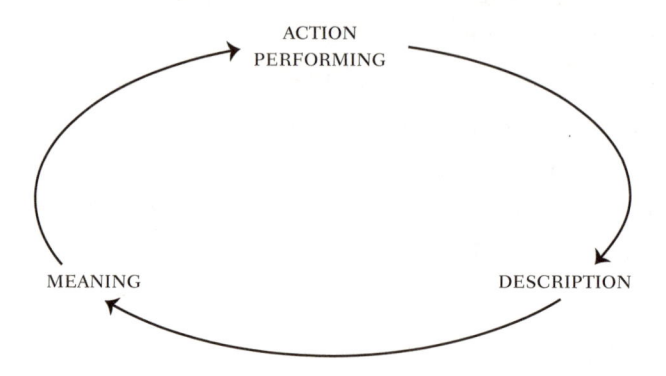

Fig. 1: The Cycle of Identity

The key here is that exceptional outcomes, such as Ryan stepping back, are examples of action in the cycle, and should be described, discussed and made meaning of, in the same way as aggressive acts are described and made meaning of. Exceptional outcomes may be acts or interactions with another, or moments of relationships that are not affected by the hostility and blame that characterise the majority of an angry adolescent's social relations. Continual discussion of such exceptional events can be a powerful force, allowing adolescents to reshape and change their social relations. The emphasis here is on helping an adolescent become able to listen to himself, and recognise himself and his achievements. This is different from having a parent, teacher, or other adult recognise him and his achievements.

All this can form part of a project by an adult to help a boy avoid being continually tossed on the sea of fate, perpetually crossed by others' intentions and actions, without any sense of how the boy might be able to shape and change his own world. Rather than leaving an adolescent powerless to recognise what he might do in the face of events, conversations over this cycle help adolescents to be able to learn on the basis of their own actions. *The boy's own words turn his anger into productive actions.*

Following the Cycle

The cycle is one that can be followed many times over successive events and incidents, in order to give a boy the ability to recognise himself, his difficulties, his limitations, his achievements, where his own moral groundings lie and therefore the limits to his aggressive acts. To summarise:

- Repeated discussions and meaning-making between an adult and a boy influence the manner in which his inner experience influences action.
- Early discussion may help the aggressive boy insert a pause for reflection between feeling and acting, for example.
- Repeated discussions about the experience of anger and perpetration of aggression help the boy to separate himself from the problem, to the point where he is able to be more self-conscious and his responses less automatic when he is angry.
- Once the boy has managed to loosen the ties between his feelings and action, the adult can initiate discussions about rules—ethical behaviour—and how aggression is perceived by others, and the implications these have on a boy's reputation.
- Adults should encourage the discussion of multiple meanings of a situation, act or relationship, rather than allow only a boy's blinkered view of the problem.
- The result is often a boy articulating examples of exceptional outcomes, where he has acted in a manner that could not be predicted from prior behaviour or reputation.

- These exceptional outcomes can be taken up once again by the adult (and at times the adolescent) as another example of action which needs to be described and made meaning of.

Such a conversation, it could be said, is interminable, between parent and child, teacher and child, a conversation that the adolescent, now a man, can continue long after the teacher or parent has moved on. Essentially, what is happening here is that the adult is assisting the boy to grasp a sense of his own emerging identity.

In adolescence, a gain or insight in one area often has cascading implications in other areas of a boy's life. For example, many boys whom I have worked with to change behaviour at school have managed to also change matters in their relationships with their families. It is quite common for the parents of such boys to report substantial improvement in communication and social exchanges at home. The transformations of a boy's inner landscape through meaning-making can move across multiple areas of his life.

We know that identity development is one of the so-called key tasks of adolescence. In adolescence there is a relative fluidity of self-awareness and identity: adolescents are always 'trying things on'. The techniques discussed in this chapter are a useful way to help all adolescents, not just angry and aggressive ones, discuss their experiences as they move through social groups, conflicts, victories and losses, as they try to find out who they are and what their future directions might be. The aim of adult involvement is not to reach a fixed formation of identity, but to help the young person find his or her way through the slings and arrows of adolescence, so they can emerge in their early twenties relatively unscathed and with some prospects.

All of this, it should be said, happens naturally between many parents and their children, between many teachers and their students. The process of imparting goals, idealism, wisdom and the like is as old as humanity and ensures the continuation of our cultural heritage. There is, however, in aggression and anger, a process that distances the angered person from access to such relationships. In continually blaming others, the boy distances himself from those very people who are best able to show him the manner in which he might be able to escape his persecutory prison.

How Does this Model Help?

The three-level model of intervention, Doing Anger Differently, may seem naively simple. However, an adult who follows the steps can help an adolescent to find a way out of his prison of persecution and into a life which is more or less directed by himself. Parents will be motivated by the fact that their son, their own flesh and blood, requires help. Teachers will be able to see some qualities in a 'difficult boy' whom they wish to help. In some cases, mentors—paid or not, who choose to spend time with troubled young people—can use such an approach. But I must emphasise that the task of assisting an adolescent to negotiate adolescence successfully is not easy or simple, and requires significant investment of time and energy.

I have summarised below some of the factors that must be remembered when utilising the approach.

Placing into Speech

Much of anger and aggression is the product of hidden ideas and half-secret emotions (latent meanings) that are outside normal consciousness, yet nonetheless exist and cause tension in the boy. Aggression physically gives expression to these hidden tendencies. Speaking about the hidden ideas and automatic understandings that give rise to aggression and that are outside the normal area of a boy's speech is difficult and time-consuming. However, ensuring they are spoken about is an important task. The effects of getting a boy to talk about the 'latent meanings' are varied, often unexpected and rarely immediately apparent. Such talk often has the quality of discovery. I have called the boy's attempts to take account of such buried understandings 'performing-meaning'. Civilisation was born when the member of one tribe hurled insults rather than a spear at a member of a rival tribe. Adolescence can be seen as a time when a boy moves from the savagery of childhood to the civility of adulthood. Speech aids this process: the power of a boy using words rather than fists is hard to underestimate.

Detailed and Nuanced Understandings

Aggressive adolescents tend to be selectively vague about the details of many situations, and 'fit' situations into pre-formed ideas. For example, Ryan easily found bossiness and persecution in what could have been Mr Johnson's attempts to help him. It probably involved a selection of details that were made into general ideas about Mr Johnson. The focus on re-description, talking things through more than once, prevents such a selective abstraction by presenting other descriptions and meanings to a boy. It raises questions about the truth that a boy may hold about anger and aggression-inducing situations.

Creating Uncertainty

As discussed earlier, the aggressive meaning creates a certainty that is unusually resistant to modification. The first step is to always clarify an individual's subjective perception of an event. This can then allow the adult to encourage other, contrasting meanings to emerge. An adult can ask questions, create a gap in an aggressive boy's iron-clad ideas about the likelihood of persecution. The purpose of creating this gap is to raise questions that arise from the discrepancies that occur when these gaps are identified. The questions will lead the boy to search for other meanings. The questions replace the certainties that are provided by the aggressive meanings.

Development of Mental Competence

The Doing Anger Differently approach makes use of, shapes and enhances the developing mental competence of adolescence. The greatest benefit is when adolescents are in relationships with people who encourage multiple viewpoints. Adults should avoid mixing authority (that is, trying to impose a meaning) and conversational (that is, trying to elicit meaning) roles, as these produce contrary effects. Authority does not result in productive conversation. As much as possible, where power relations develop or are inevitable, these situations should be talked about. A focus here is to convert power relations into communication.

Moral Development

Adults can also use the Doing Anger Differently approach as a method of drawing out moral values from the boy with the idea that moral thought may lead to moral action. There are problems associated with teaching or transmitting morality in adolescence, particularly with angry adolescents: both the influence of the peer group and rejection of adult authority mean that although a level of moral reasoning may be attained, moral action may not accompany it. Placing adolescents in the role of ethicists of their own environment will mean that any moral values they adopt will have greater influence on their actions.

Using the 'Doing–Being' of Adolescence

As I have emphasised, in adolescence, to a greater extent than in later life, learning occurs through experience rather than merely mental reflection. Though all humans act out their emotions without fully understanding them, action is an important and useful form of communication for adolescents and children, which needs to be taken up and worked with. Adolescents need help to interpret their actions, which in turn assists adolescents to put their actions into words, a fundamental failure in the case of reactive aggression. If an adult can help an adolescent to begin to talk through his experiences, this inclines the adolescent towards speaking about his feelings, giving them shape and structure, rather than acting impulsively upon emotion.

In Brief

- Parents and adults in contact with an aggressive boy are in a key position to discuss and shape the emerging meanings he places on events.

- Parents and other adults can assist with the development of meaning-making abilities of adolescents by taking up certain positions, which may change depending on the difficulties with which the adolescent is struggling.

- A fundamental method of gaining knowledge and insight in adolescence is 'doing–being', which is midway between the child's play and the adult's intellectual reflection.

- Parents and adults working with angry boys can use the method of 'doing–being' to help shape their emotional, intellectual and moral development.

- Parents and adults should see their role as that of an 'intellectual midwife'. Adults should try to be involved in an ongoing conversation with an adolescent, which on the one hand allows room for him to find his own way, yet gently questions or pushes him; the adults' approach should be based on what they have observed in the boy's behaviour and responses, and have spoken with him about in the past.

- There are three crucial points in this intellectual midwife approach: looking at the level of *perception and description*—what the adolescent 'leaves out'; listening and talking at the level of *meaning-making*—the specific types of meaning that an adolescent endorses and espouses; and looking and listening at the level of *performing-meaning*—what the adolescent does based on these meanings, particularly those positive acts which he himself cannot recognise. Discussions at these multiple levels are aimed at assisting the adolescent move beyond the simple inference of 'he hurt me, therefore I hurt will hurt him' to a more sophisticated understanding of his role in his relationships.

- Create questions and doubts, rather than certainties.
- As much as possible, don't lecture an adolescent at length. If something is not allowed, simply tell him and await his response. If an issue needs to be discussed, discuss it. Lecturing is simply a means of the parent attempting to enforce his or her worldview on an adolescent.

6
What Parents Can Do: Techniques for Intervening with an Angry Adolescent

In this chapter I will outline four techniques for directly intervening with an angry adolescent. These techniques are designed for situations where an adult:

- is faced with intervening in an angry or aggressive conflict;
- has decided to raise the problem of the conflict later on;
- is looking to make peace after a conflict;
- needs to prevent conflicts from spiralling into more anger and aggression.

I also discuss how to turn the problem of these conflicts into a 'crisis of possibility'—helping a boy to make plans for what he wishes to achieve in the future.

I will use the example of one family to illustrate all of these techniques. I first discussed the family in the Introduction to this book, where Charles showed aggression when asked to do homework rather than play his electronic game. Charles was coming towards the end of Year 7 when that incident occurred. His mother, Tania, was understandably very upset about the argument with her son.

Constructive Conflict: Turning Crises into Questions

I wish to emphasise that verbal communication during an angry conflict can be productive, as well as more thoughtful discussion after the conflict is over. Communication while a boy is angry and the reflection about anger in a calm moment are two different ways of looking at conflict. They often yield different information and ideas. These differing perspectives in turn yield clues about the problems underlying the anger. The heat of anger often allows something to be said that would not otherwise be uttered and often some of the best understandings are yielded during and straight after an angry or aggressive conflict. These can be discussed as part of a series of problems and questions that the boy's anger raises.

> Tania and her two children, Charles, aged 13, and Sabina, 15, had just arrived home. Tania had picked up the teenagers from school on the way home from her job as an advertising executive. Tania was tired, as she had been working particularly long hours: she had an important project to finish, which involved her leaving home at 5.30 a.m., while her husband, Peter, had to take the children to school. Peter often had to work late because of the later start he made after dropping off the children. Tania had been feeling that she had 'lost touch' a little with her children, despite her best attempts.
>
> On this night a fight broke out between Charles and Sabina. Tania had noticed that the fighting between her children had become worse, just at the time when she was busy, tired and stressed at work. It was coming to the end of a long year and Tania was looking forward to a holiday.

Tania went into the lounge, where Charles and Sabina were yelling at each other. Charles had been playing his Xbox on the TV when Sabina had wanted to watch a DVD of video hits her father had recorded for her on the weekend. As Tania walked in, Charles was yelling: 'I'm sick of you wanting to watch your stupid girlie crap on the TV. I want to play, now give it back.' He tried to snatch the Xbox controller from Sabina, but ended up hitting her over the shoulder as Sabina pulled it out of Charles's reach. Still gripping the controller, Sabina fell to the floor, knocking her head on the side of the couch. Charles, a little taken aback by his sister's fall, then took a step towards her as if to grab the controller.

Tania walked over and placed herself between the two teenagers, and although she felt like screaming at them both, helped Sabina up, placed her at one end of the couch and asked Charles to sit down at the other end. On similar occasions previously, Tania had simply confiscated the Xbox and forbidden the use of the TV. However, she had talked to Peter the night before about the escalating conflict between the two children, and had decided that it was time to help them talk about it.

Tania asked: 'What's going on?'

Sabina responded immediately, with tears streaming down her face, 'He hit me! And he pushed me over so I hit my head on the couch! He's turned into a real little bastard lately, and all I wanted to do was to watch the videos Dad gave me, and I haven't had a chance because he's been playing his stupid games.' Sabina turned to Charles, and said tauntingly, 'You know you're not allowed to hit. There's no violence allowed in the house! When Dad gets home you're going to get it!'

Tania then turned to Charles and asked, 'What about you, Charles, what happened?'

What Parents Can Do

Whenever Sabina interrupted, she asked Sabina to wait until Charles had finished speaking. Clearly less articulate than his sister, Charles said, 'I just wanted to play on the Xbox for half an hour. She can't come in and kick me off.'

Sabina: 'You hit me, you hit me!! You're going to get it!!'

Charles (getting angrier): 'I didn't! I didn't hit you! I was just trying to get the controller!'

After this went on for a little while, it became clear to Tania that the children needed some extra help to resolve the conflict, as they were both solidifying their positions, with Charles denying what he had actually done, however accidental it was, and Sabina attempting to provoke him more and more. Tania said, 'Charles, I did see your arm make contact with Sabina. Maybe you mean you didn't mean to hit her.'

Charles: 'No, I didn't mean it!!'

Sabina (in a sing-song): 'You're going to get it, you're going to get it!'

Tania: 'Sabina, did you hear what Charles said? He said he didn't mean to hit you.'

Sabina: 'But he still did, and that's against the rules!'

Tania: 'Well, to be violent you actually have to mean to cause harm and I'm not sure that's true, given what Charles just said …'

Charles: 'She shouldn't have snatched the controller from me!'

Sabina: 'I had to, you idiot, because you had those stupid headphones on and you were ignoring me.'

At this point, Charles and Sabina have moved back and forth several times between description and meaning: what actually happened and what the meanings of the happenings were. Though this has occurred in an argumentative manner, such a discussion probably would not have been possible even half an hour later, as the two children would have calmed down and wouldn't have wanted to speak about the problem any more. The problem would have been 'swept under the carpet', but a bubbling resentment between the siblings would remain, ready to be ignited at the next disagreement.

Even in the aftermath of a fight, Tania is helping her children try to reckon with the rules of the house and decide whether something is okay or not. Rather than imposing a rule, she is helping them find a compromise within the rules. This eventually bore fruit, as Sabina and Charles agreed to half-hour shifts on the TV after they arrived home from school each night, and they agreed they could swap which one of them had first turn.

Tania also knew that there were two further problems, even though peace had been made: Sabina's outrage at being struck by Charles, and Sabina's taunting of Charles that he was 'going to get it' from his father. In order to deal with the first problem, Tania told Charles that even though it had been accidental, he still had hit Sabina and people were normally sorry for problems they caused accidentally. Charles volunteered spontaneously that, to show he was sorry, Sabina could watch her DVD straight away.

Regarding the second problem, Tania was troubled by Sabina continually using her father's name in this manner, but she was not precisely sure why it troubled her, and thus what to do about it. She thought it was best left until she could talk with Peter about it.

Note the following points about what Tania did:

- She put aside her own frustrations, and her wish just to deal with the conflict easily and simply by 'laying down the law' (by confiscation) without discussing it. She knew from experience that 'laying down the law' would result in another night of bubbling resentment where the cauldron of emotions would not have been spoken about.
- In addition, the conflicts had been getting worse, so she decided to try something different.

- Tania used the children's responses to past interventions to guide her next move. The responses to past interventions and the parent's understanding of these responses are a better guide than rules.
- She ensured her two children were separated, so the physical conflict (although it appeared in part an accident) could not continue.
- She asked a simple question about the situation, even though it seemed very clear on one level what was going on: her children were fighting yet again! This allowed each child to state his or her position, an antidote to the cancelling out of each other's rights when it seems to the children there is not enough for both.
- She allowed Sabina, the more articulate of her children, to respond, but then gave equal time to Charles.
- She did not try to impose her reading of the situation, but gave her children the chance to air their views.
- She handed responsibility for solving the problem to her children, but remained as a presence and a guide while they sorted it out. In doing this, Tania is helping her children use words rather than actions to sort out their conflicts.
- Although she did not have to use her power as ultimate arbiter, by her presence she and her children implicitly acknowledged that she had this power, if a peaceful solution could not be found. Adolescents are still somewhat childlike, and need the support and guidance of parents in these situations.
- When she was in doubt about something (Sabina's taunting of Charles) she abstained from acting on it until she had a chance to reflect on the matter.

Tania was simply relieved that Charles's act of allowing Sabina to watch the DVD had stopped the conflict for the present. Tired from work, and glad the argument was over, she could have let the matter rest. This is what many parents do, avoiding the possibility of another angry outburst once it is over. But she was also a little surprised: over the previous few months Charles had been very angry, full of rivalry and resentful towards Sabina. Given this, his act of generosity seemed a little unusual.

> When Charles came into the kitchen to have a drink a little later, Tania asked him about it. He said, 'I realised that it didn't matter, 'cause it was just causing problems between me and her. I've got plenty of time later tonight to play on the Xbox and because she gets to play her DVD doesn't mean that I miss out.'

What is interesting about this statement is that it shows Charles had developed a reflective capacity to think outside the rivalry with his sister. He had used reason to think beyond the 'if she gets it I won't' emotional thinking promoted by anger, and realised there were more important things. Interestingly, the 'more important thing' was Charles's relationship with his sister. This also represents a significant movement: Charles had decided that his relationship with his sister was an important longer term priority, above his enjoyment in the half-hour after school. It could be a sign that Charles is ready to think and talk more about such things.

His statement also had Tania thinking about the rise in rivalry between her children, and she wondered if the fighting was not actually about material things, but caused by the fact there had been little relationship time in the house over the previous six months.

All of this took around 20 minutes—a lot longer than the option of confiscation of the Xbox and the teenagers' confinement to their bedrooms would have taken. However, the rewards for Tania were

What Parents Can Do

that the atmosphere of the house had changed considerably that evening. After similar arguments the house had been stalked by two sullen and warring teenagers. On the night of this fight, after some time had passed following the conflict, Charles sat at the kitchen bench and discussed his day at school with her and later Sabina came in, unsummoned, to ask if she could help with dinner.

Some further points:

- Tania had changed her stance in regard to her children. She had become more present to them in a way that facilitated talk about the problem. The value of this talk is not to be underestimated. Talking loosens the link between feeling and action. It also creates a structure through which siblings can negotiate their relationships.

- Adolescents still tend to 'do', rather than 'say' their distress. It is possible to see the conflict between Charles and Sabina as a symptom of the increase in stress on the part of the parents. This doesn't mean what Tania and Peter were doing is incorrect or wrong, simply that if parents don't like increased conflict in the household (I'm yet to meet a parent who explicitly says they do) then they need to find a way to become more present, to find a new stance with their children, to act. This is exactly what Tania decided to do after speaking with Peter about the increase in conflicts.

- Tania was not extravagant in her reaction. She simply asserted her presence and guided her children in accordance with the way she was reading the situation. This required her own form of restraint: laying down the law and sending her children to their rooms might have been the best way to relieve her own frustration and tension (not all of it to do with her children). However, laying down the law was not the best way to deal with this situation. Past experience told her that.

Doing Anger Differently

> That night over dinner, Tania brought up the earlier incident. She did so after discussing what had happened briefly with Peter over the phone as he was coming home. Tania raised the issue because she wanted to see how Charles and Sabina were thinking about the fight now they had calmed down a little. Tania and Peter had also agreed it was important that the children knew that he knew about the incident, as Sabina had threatened action from Peter to punish Charles for hitting her. Over dinner, Sabina chatted calmly about the fight, saying Charles had hit her but that he hadn't meant to, but Charles stayed quiet, looking down at this plate.
>
> Peter asked Charles if it was correct that he didn't mean it, and Charles replied that he hadn't meant to hurt Sabina, he just wanted his Xbox controller back. Peter made sure to say that as Charles had apologised it was okay.
>
> Tania realised that although it was late October, they had not discussed as a family their plans for the holidays. Tonight she made a point of doing this. Such a discussion about holidays created a 'family moment' where they all made a decision together, and meant the family had something which they could look forward to together.

This was another important way of responding to the earlier conflict. Sometimes the best parental responses are to not respond directly to the overt issue, but to understand the underlying issues that have led to a conflict. Tania understood that it was possible her children were fighting over scarce emotional and relationship space between the children and the parents. She realised there was little she could do in the short term about her work, but that talking about plans for a family holiday would increase the enjoyment of family life both before and during the holiday. It created a joint vision that gave the family something to do together.

Constructive Conflict: A Summary

These are the basic steps for intervening into conflict constructively.

1. Speedy Intervention

Intervening speedily into the conflict is useful. This is because conflict is a place where the problem of anger and aggression shows itself most clearly—at the time when the emotion has erupted. If too much time is left after the event, participants in conflicts tend to 'sweep the problem under the carpet', and are reluctant to let the problem rise again. People have a tendency towards self-preservation and avoidance of continual outright conflict, which means that it may be difficult to discuss an issue once the heat has gone out of the problem.

2. Intervention Steps

An adult should drop what they are doing and fully attend to the problem that has emerged. Initially:

- Allow emotions to fester until they are undeniable, but intervene early if it is clear there is a developing tension in the family or group of adolescents.

- *Physically separate* the parties to the conflict if there has been physical contact, to ensure safety.

- Take up the position of *consultant*, not necessarily rescuing one of the combatants in order to make the situation tolerable.

- Being a consultant means simply assisting a teenager to say what led to the conflict. Follow the techniques set out in Chapter 5.

- *Elicit descriptions*: ask the combatants to describe what happened, initially focusing on actions, but attempt to move the discussion on by asking them to reveal internal feelings and opinions. The involvement of other witnesses to the conflict in reaching a description may be helpful.

- Don't be dragged at this stage into arguing what the anger is about. A boy may have chosen to express anger because it is the safest emotion to express at that moment. Accept his assertions at this stage. Latent meanings can be discussed later.

- Early on, it may be enough for a boy merely to have his internal state spoken about. Clearly allowing a boy to express his view of what happened may achieve a lot. This sends a message to him that negative emotions are not 'bad' or 'wrong' but will be tolerated. Over time this can give a boy the capacity to tolerate his negative emotions, as they have been validated and tolerated by an adult. This leads to less impulsiveness and a search for alternative ways of responding to these emotions.

- Later, it may be important to communicate that it is the boy's aggressive actions that are not being tolerated.

- *Meanings*: elicit the reasons and justifications that lie behind the aggressive action. Do not directly challenge or disparage any meaning that may be put.

- *Contrast* these whys of aggression with the goals the boy may have. Move between the little picture of the conflict and the big picture of a boy's wishes and goals for his schooling, employment, relationships, or some views that the boy may have expressed in regard to some moral code. This *pointing to contradictions* may become easier as the techniques are used more often. Pointing to contradictions may also be best left until after the conflict-ridden atmosphere has eased.

- Do not be afraid to place a boy who frequently utilises aggression in an uncomfortable position. Encourage others who may be there to express a viewpoint on the conflict, thus allowing multiple perspectives.

- If a boy has been treated unfairly (however out of proportion his actions seem) support him by helping him to speak further about what has been unfair.

- Equally, be careful not to encourage a boy's 'poor-me' view of the world. Once the unfairness has been acknowledged, gently start to challenge ideas, however latent, that keep a boy frozen within passive victim-hood.

- The *exception* to this consultative or coaching position is when a young person may be at physical or emotional risk. Here, adults should intervene in whatever way is necessary to ensure physical and psychical safety.

3. Further Key Points

- Constructive conflict intervention is not an easy technique to implement—it tests the creativity and patience of the adults involved—but it is generally transforming for boys with the correct safeguards.

- This technique amounts to an attempt to replace the certainty of the 'It's not fair' of anger and aggression with questions and doubt.

- It is done by contrasting the meanings the boy discusses in the conflict with his other goals and aims, moral values.

- Don't insist on a meaning. Suggest, talk about, but don't attempt to enforce.

- Be curious. Remember to show as well as tell. Be open to a boy's ideas and incorporate these into the discussion.

Constructive Contemplation: Helping a Boy Reflect on Anger

When a conflict is not occurring there may be opportunities for adults and adolescents to reflect on the problems of conflicts.

At such times, the problem can be approached in a manner that makes it clear to the adolescent that the adult is not being punitive. However, it is almost inevitable (initially at least) that adolescents will expect unpleasant consequences once the issue of their conflict and aggression is raised. This seemed to be a reaction Charles was showing when the fight was raised over dinner.

Talking about displays of anger can lead anywhere. Recall that in Chapter 1 I discussed how anger is often the tip of an iceberg. Without the pressure of anger and hostility present, it may be possible to discuss what lies behind the anger, something seldom possible during an angry episode.

> Peter and Charles had the opportunity to talk further the next day when they went shopping; Peter arranged this as he had wanted to make sure that he talked more with Charles. During the conversation, Peter picked up the thread of what Tania had told him: that Charles had let Sabina have the TV to resolve the conflict. Peter asked Charles about this. Charles replied that although he hadn't meant to hurt Sabina, when he was angry he just didn't care whether he hurt her or not, and when he had calmed down a little, he felt bad about the fact he had hit her and he let her use the TV to show that he did care.
>
> Peter followed this up, trying to tease out the importance of the relationship above Charles simply getting what he wanted. They also discussed the problem of giving up something and the problem of the anger that might remain. Peter then moved from the picture of the family to Charles's life at school, asking, 'Are there other people with whom you feel your anger is causing problems?' Charles replied that there had been a few girls at school where it had been the case, and that many of the girls didn't like him, because they thought he was an angry person. Peter asked how long this had been going on,

and Charles answered for about 18 months. Peter realised this was quite soon after the family had lost their house in a sudden and catastrophic bushfire. No one in the family had been hurt physically, but of all the family, Charles had lost the most, as his room had been completely destroyed. Rather than pursue that, Peter decided to take up the problem of here and now.

Peter asked Charles what he was doing now, when the girls made him angry. Charles said, 'Oh, I'm walking away'. Now this was a start, in that Charles wasn't doing anything to damage the relationships further, and walking away showed a degree of emotional containment. However, Peter was worried that girls had become a sort of mental punching bag for Charles: if he was upset, then he became angry at women around him. He wondered vaguely about how Charles and Sabina had nearly always fought from the time Charles could stand up, and whether this had set up some type of model in Charles's mind. He realised these were his worries, and decided not to talk about them with Charles just yet, but to wait and see how the situation developed, because he wasn't sure how far this problem extended beyond his own worries.

Peter asked if Charles liked being angry with the girls at school. Charles replied that he didn't, but he said that it was how most of his male friends treated girls: 'Like they are idiots who don't know anything'. Peter asked what Charles's best friend Robbie thought about all of this: 'Robbie sort of plays along with the guys in our group at school when he's with them but he told me that he really likes a girl in the year above us'. [This is an example of asking about another's perspective in order to discover a new meaning or perspective.]

Charles went on to say that he was finding that many of the girls at school he had been angry at 'I also sort of like. It's like now I'm pretending to be angry whereas in primary

> school the boys didn't really hang around with the girls.' Peter asked what he liked about these girls, and Charles answered: 'I like how they're not scared to come up and talk to us, even though some of the girls don't like me or some of the guys in my group. It's like they don't care what others think.' Peter asked if some of the guys in Charles's year had started going out with girls, which Charles confirmed. Peter said, 'Sounds like you might like to talk with these girls a bit more, and not be worried too much by what the other guys think.' Later still, Peter simply said what Charles was on the verge of thinking anyway: 'I wonder how you are going to get these girls to see you differently?'
>
> In a conversation some weeks later, Charles told Peter that he had found a way. He said his problem with the girls had been that he thought they thought they were better than all the guys. In his words, 'Heaps of girls are snobs'. He had found that girls treated him differently if he didn't respond angrily, but he tried to 'out-snob them'. All of a sudden, Charles found, girls treated him differently, and began to talk to him more.

Over this time, Peter was helping Charles in several ways. In the language I was using in Chapter 5, he was expanding on what was an exceptional outcome that could not have been predicted by Charles's behaviour towards Sabina in the previous months. In addition:

- He was helping his son give shape to his emerging realisation about the importance of relationships. As Charles talked about it, it gave rise to a value or belief that he could carry with him. This is the core of a parent's 'midwife' stance: assisting a boy to give birth to ideas that are nonetheless the boy's own. Certainly, this idea about relationships with girls was latent within Charles's original statement to Tania.

What Parents Can Do

- Peter used the perspective of Charles's friends to create new possibilities. Friends can be, but don't have to be, present for this to happen.

- By returning to talk and question his son again and again, Peter helped him explore something that Charles could not do by himself: address the difficulties that lay behind the small part of the anger iceberg that was visible. There were few signs that the original conflict with Sabina could have led, over a period of weeks, to a discussion about 'snobby girls'.

- There was a crisis of possibility (see below) for Charles in regard to his relationships with girls. Once Charles realised he wanted something more from girls, he was able to change how he acted towards them. Note that Peter chose his moment to say this, waiting until Charles was nearly ready with his own realisation. Nor did Peter speak about his own worries about women functioning for Charles as a 'mental punching bag'. In this way, Charles took the crisis as his own and was able to act on it.

- Within this crisis, Peter helped Charles listen to himself, rather than simply going along with his group of friends. As a result he came up with his own solution (however temporary) to the crisis.

- Peter realised that the house fire where Charles lost all of his belongings probably explained some of Charles's anger. If one loses everything, one might be fiercely protective of possessions. This point may be important to talk about in another moment, but Peter stayed focused in the here and now, and the problem of the relationships Charles was having with girls. This was far more likely to provoke a crisis and give Charles a reason to change his response to anger than the loss of his possessions. The latter would be likely to provoke a 'poor-me' stance, which might rob Charles of a sense of his ability to act for himself.

- Peter also has faith that what he says and does with his son is important. That Peter thinks words mean something, have a weight and a lasting effect is shown by his attentive listening to Charles and the careful choice of his words.

- Peter was helping Charles with one of the 'natural crises' of adolescence, the fact of sexual maturity. He was engaging in an ongoing discussion that allowed his son to find his own way to negotiate his path, but also gave him guidance along the way. Whatever one might think of Charles's tactic of 'out-snobbing' it was his solution, and this is what gives the solution its value. It seemed to work, for the time being, but probably comes with its own problems, to be taken up and wrestled with in the future.

- By this stage, Peter and Tania have, through dialogue with their son, successfully turned the conflict with Sabina into a series of questions which Charles thinks about and addresses.

This is an example of how, if such an approach is applied over time, parents can aid and abet the increasing emotional sophistication of adolescence.

Constructive Contemplation: A Summary

Here are some simple steps to ensure these more reflective times can be constructive and not turn into another conflict.

1. Recognise the Kernel of Truth

- Boys commonly expect punishment and disparagement once a 'difficult issue' is raised. Predict and counteract the inevitable defensiveness (see 'I am not wrong about myself', page 14). Although the temptation to blame a boy for his aggressive acts will often be very strong, if progress is to be made on discussing the problem, he should not (at least initially) be blamed.

What Parents Can Do

- Work to find and recognise the kernel of truth in the boy's actions during the conflict. At first, speaking of the internal state that brought the disruptive act(s) should be prioritised over discussing the acts themselves. For example, a parent or teacher might say to a boy who swore at a teacher and was sent out of class: 'It sounds like something got you pretty upset in Mr Smith's class yesterday. I wonder why that was?' An educated guess about the internal experience of a boy may be necessary, as he may not be able to describe how he felt before the incident. The guess is a reading of the boy's behaviour (if an adult was there to witness it) or statements (if the adult is listening to the boy describe the incident) the boy has made. Tania 'read' Charles's behaviour by wondering about his allowing Sabina to use the television. This in turn revealed his 'feeling bad', opening up a whole area of discussion that would not have occurred otherwise. Behind such small acts can lie great tracts of revelation.

- Again, the stance is that of a midwife. The adult is beside the boy, as an ally, helping the boy draw out the knowledge and lessons from the latest problem. Many boys are surprised by this stance, and this surprise means the moment of reflection can be one of profound difference. The difference that the adult seeks is for the boy to put a name to and speak about the circumstances of his inner experience, rather than acting it out, or defending his actions.

- More latent meanings can be guessed at, or wondered about, or pursued once a boy is no longer angry and is less defensive. These meanings can be developed gradually (and never enforced) over a number of conversations, as Peter did with Charles.

- Remember that anger is often the tip of the iceberg, with a myriad other responses and recollections lying submerged below the tip.

These submerged portions can emerge during discussions in more reflective times.

2. Action

Once a boy has acknowledged his internal experience, only then can discussion move on. There are many possible paths to follow, depending on the situation, and below I outline a few.

- The nature of the problem can be discussed on the boy's terms, which may involve a move from the small detail of today to the larger, less certain canvas of the future. Possible changes in behaviour, different mental approaches can be discussed. It is best if these ideas come from the boy, but he may need some help. Adults can offer to help with the change but Peter chose simply to lay the challenge of his behaviour at Charles's feet: 'I wonder how you are going to …'

- It is important NOT TO accept a boy's guarantees when he is not angry that he can easily achieve something (for example, 'Yeah, I can just walk away' or 'I can keep my mouth shut in Mr Smith's class'). This is what Peter did with Charles's 'I walk away from the girls'.

- Don't just outline the problem, but also offer a boy assistance to fix the problem, if necessary. The sort of help an angry boy might need could be help with organising a meeting or mediation with another boy who has caused recurring problems at school, or to give reminders in the family or class about agreements, or to assist with a boy's monitoring of his anger levels, or to offer to raise a problem with another family member so it can be discussed, or simply to remain open and question a boy about how he is going on a regular basis.

- However, this assistance may not always be necessary. One way of judging this is the degree to which a boy's words have matched his actions in the past. I once worked with a boy who had problems getting to school on time. Despite persistent problems, he told me one day out of the blue that he felt he could do it. I took this at face value, rather than problem solve it with him, because I had noticed in the past that everything he had told me he would do he had done. Sure enough, he made it to school on time, and we were able to discuss how he did this in the light of his success.

- It may be important to discuss the means by which the boy could repair the damage caused by the conflict, by words or action (this is what Charles did by letting Sabina have the TV). Helping a boy with reparation tends to halt the cycle of anger and remorse that many angry boys are trapped in. It is best to allow the boy the chance to look at his regret about the incident and find his own means of repairing the damage (given this has happened, what do you most want to change/what do you feel most bad about?).

3. Assistance

It is important that an adult seeks to help the boy by whatever means agreed to in the moment of reflection. *The adult must stick to the agreement*, even if the boy does not keep his part of the bargain. For example, I offered to help a boy in a group I was conducting at a school raise an issue of being called names by his friends. I stuck by this even though the boy himself starting calling his persecutors names when he entered a room after I had been speaking with him.

Making Peace: Reading the Signs

> Tania and Charles were having an argument about his attendance at school one morning. The argument had continued for more than an hour, with Tania worried about her son's increasing difficulty with going to school. She wanted to make a stand on this morning when it was clear to her that her son was not physically sick. However, when it was time for Charles to leave

> for school, while he might not have been sick, his distress from the argument meant that he was emotionally not well enough to go. Tania let Charles stay home, on the stipulation that he stay in his room, work on his assignments and not go out. On her return home from work, Tania found herself still angry with her son from the morning, but that he had been obedient to her wishes. Charles was silent and sullen.

Many parents find it difficult to know what to do about a resentful atmosphere. Misunderstandings and anger can be called forth easily, as neither side is sure of the other's motives and are attuned to look for signs of ill-will. In an atmosphere like this it is the parent's role to take the first step. This is what Tania did.

> Tania asked Charles if he had any objections to what she had planned for dinner that night and added she was going to the supermarket to buy the ingredients. She asked Charles to do five household tasks while she was gone, and emphasised that she expected them completed when she returned. While she was at the supermarket, Tania received a text from Charles asking if she could get some of his favourite dessert. Tania texted back her assent. On her return, Tania found that the tasks had been done. She thanked Charles warmly for doing them and talked about how delicious dinner was going to be that night. Tania found that Charles was far less silent and sullen, and wanting to talk about the assignment he had been trying to complete that day and his plans for the rest of the year.

One thing that is clear from this story is that Tania knew how to end an argument without giving up too much ground on the boundaries she thought important to enforce. She was flexible in realising that more harm than good would be done by rigidly enforcing her wish that Charles go to school that day. However, in giving in to his demand to stay at home, Tania made sure that there were certain restrictions that Charles had to keep to. In giving in she did not give up everything.

Second, she also ensured, on arriving home, that she gave her son a task to perform so that he could win back her goodwill. She asked him to do something that meant that he could receive thanks from her when she arrived home from shopping. Most importantly, Tania was also able to read the peace signs. Rather than being indignant about the request for a favourite dessert (for instance, thinking: 'He's been home all day slacking off! What's he done to earn his favourite dessert?') she saw it was an opportunity to mend the relationship.

The important point is that there are often many ways to show goodwill and open a boy to showing goodwill which don't mean giving up a stance on an important issue.

Cutting Across the Imaginary Contagion and Escalation of Anger

Where there is ongoing conflict with an adolescent, commonly:

- the boy's silence is read as anger by the adult;
- the adult avoids eye contact with the boy ('I'm sick of his outbursts');
- the boy in turn reads this as a sign that the adult is angry with him;
- at this stage the slightest accident or misconstrued word can set off the argument again.

The latest round of conflict will have been caused by what one party has imagined about the other. There has been no actual conflict about an issue, but a conflict which is the product of an *ongoing mutual suspicion*. Tania's clear directions to Charles (and Charles's request for the dessert) cut across this escalation and repaired the situation.

The use of words and the setting of structure is a powerful tool that the adult (as the more mature and powerful of the pair) can use to defuse the situation. Here are some tips to defuse this suspicion.

- Use words. If there is tension in the air as a result of an earlier argument, speak about something that gives an indication of your goodwill, or something that will involve a lessening of the conflict. It may be worthwhile saying: 'That was a bad fight we had this morning. I'm not angry about it now.'
- If you find yourself being suspicious, looking for faults, or for signs of ill-will in your son, stop it.
- Try to break the tense silence with an offering about your day, or question your son. 'How was school today?' 'How did you go with that homework?'
- Give a boy a structure as a means of demonstrating his goodwill, as Tania did with Charles by setting him tasks to do while she was out at the shop.
- Call in a third person. If you are parenting by yourself, or in a one-on-one situation with the boy, as a teacher or youth worker, it may be important at times to call in a close family friend or someone whom the boy knows well. This third person can offer a place for the boy to talk about the conflict, and can explain something that gets around the suspicion that may have pervaded a relationship. This third person can also be a therapist: steps for finding a therapist are discussed in the Appendix.

Identifying Crises of Possibility

Most parents, teachers and youth workers see recurring problems with anger and aggression as a crisis which requires the young person to change his behaviour. This is probably accurate. However, a young person may need a reason to change. Talking with a young adolescent

What Parents Can Do

about how his behaviour makes life difficult and upsetting for siblings, classmates or teachers may have little impact. Why should he give up acting this way when it makes perfect sense to him that he is acting in the only manner he can?

What may be more constructive is to use the manner in which an adolescent behaves, and the reactions of those around him (that is, school disciplinary actions, withdrawal of friendships, suspensions from sporting associations, etc.) *to create a 'crisis of possibility' in regard to what he wants to be*. This is a way of working with an adolescent that presents the problems of his behaviour precisely on his own terms. It is to be preferred to limiting an adolescent's behaviour via the imposition of authority or wisdom handed down from on high. Resorting to either of these methods often produces a reaction that is contrary to the aims of the adult (but note that the use of authority is vital in some situations). Helping an adolescent by offering concrete steps to put things right may only be useful once a young person understands the full enormity of the crisis. How can a young person realise this? It may take actual sanctions by authorities such as the school, a parent or people that the adolescent likes and wants to be with, before he makes a start on accepting the problem.

In the discussions between Peter and Charles, this is what happened. Charles's problems at home were linked to his difficulties at school, and the discussion was able to produce a crisis in regard to relationships that meant Charles could see what was in it for him to change his anger.

It should be kept in mind that all of the techniques outlined in this chapter have two aims.

- First, dealing with the immediate problem of the conflict in the present. This is the problem that many parents, teachers and other professionals get 'caught within'. Having an angry boy in a house or within a class tends to raise everyone's background level of anger and propensity to aggressiveness. Dealing with this may involve managing or containing the distress, damage and difficulty provoked in a boy and those around him by the expression of anger and aggression.

- Second, to use these techniques (if necessary) repetitively, adjusted to each new context, in order to help a boy understand more deeply the problem of his anger and work towards changing his anger and aggression in line with what he wants to achieve. The three antidotes of reflection, relationships and ability to act independently should be kept in mind here. As discussed in Part I, aggressive adolescent boys have difficulty accepting limits with their long-term best interests in mind. If an adolescent cannot do this, then an adult must. Use the big three to do this.

Recall the video of the giant hands that I discussed in Chapter 2. The hands of the law become permeable and provisional in adolescence. The position of the parents is to help an adolescent find where these giant hands of the law lie for him. To do this is to help a boy find a freedom, as the hands become less permeable. This is because the hands are no longer those of the parent, the school or some outside authority. The hands are an implication of what an adolescent wants for himself.

Paths to Maturity: Making Plans

It is important, once a crisis of possibility has emerged in discussion with an adolescent, not to then leave him to his own devices. 'I think he has finally got it' the adult might think to him- or herself. However, it is likely that a young person will still need help and support in his struggles with the day-to-day minutiae of achieving something of his 'wish-to-be'. Break big wishes and goals down into smaller chunks. Recognise a boy's achievements based on previous discussions.

This is exactly what Peter did by revisiting the discussion several times with Charles in the weeks after the fight. This helped Charles enormously in structuring his own world.

7
What Adults Can Do: Principles for Intervening with an Adolescent

The techniques outlined in the previous chapter have limits to their usefulness. Any technique, as a description of various actions an adult might perform, has limits if the broader context of the adolescent's situation is ignored. Adults who can put into action broader principles without the detail of techniques will just as likely see results as favourable as if the techniques are followed assiduously. Rigidly following techniques without regard to the wider context will be unlikely to have favourable results, as this would be to follow a technique without listening to the adolescent.

In this chapter I therefore outline what I think are some of the fundamental principles to hold in mind when intervening with an angry adolescent. Perhaps the two most important are 'antidotes to anger' and 'showing as well as telling'. Holding these principles in your mind when dealing with angry adolescents may well be enough to assist a boy to work through his anger difficulties.

Giving a boy, for example, a 'pat on the back', simply recognising the positives in his carrying out something well, will mean little and have little effect if his means of achieving the outcome are ignored. In addition, trying a technique like this only once will also have little effect. An understanding of the broader picture is necessary to sustain continued effort. The broader picture is certainly something that Peter is attending to when he speaks with Charles, although his comments are sparse.

Using Antidotes to Anger

All the case studies I have discussed so far have featured, one way or another, the three interlinked antidotes to anger (see Chapter 5). These are the three core mental activities that are destroyed or inhibited by anger and a paranoid habit of mind: attending to relationships, reflection and autonomous action. Enhancing a boy's attention to his relationships (including the relationship he has with himself), improving his capacity to reflect on social situations and enhancing his ability to act for himself, towards his own goals, will all assist in the problems that anger causes.

For Alan (see page 13), in the moment of his persecution, his relationship to his classmates mattered little and he was unable to reflect on the meaning of his act. He simply had to destroy those taunting him. He also perplexed the school authorities as he seemed incapable of holding to a plan of action or agreement, such as, 'I want to stay at school, therefore I won't hit others'. He could not follow the plan, although he accepted it was in his interests. His permeability precluded a direction, lessening his ability to act for himself. He merely shifted in accordance with the demands of each situation.

In John's case, he was directed by the short-term gains of enjoying how his friends saw him as someone who didn't care about rules. In our work together and with discussions with his family he came to see the importance of his relationship with the school and teachers, began to be able to reflect and work on this relationship and took matters into his own hands, leaving and returning to his school. His case shows how it is possible for an adolescent to move positions from victim to an individual in charge of his actions, with quite a dramatic difference in outcome.

What Adults Can Do

For Douglas (see page 52), an ability to act independently, reflection and attention to relationships were all present in varying degrees, but he found it difficult to have them all together. Despite his success as an academic (which clearly shows a high degree of self-directed action) he wished to isolate himself from his colleagues, always carrying on battles with them inside and outside his head. He was also bent on trying to find a father figure that could guarantee or fix something in his life. In this way, although he certainly had some degree of agency, he always directed his actions at the behest of some imagined other person. The continual performing for others deafened Douglas to himself, lessening his ability to act independently.

Perhaps Greg's case (see page 66) shows the inevitability that our actions are always at the behest of some internalised other person. However, Greg showed how it is possible to evade a fate that he clearly stated he did not wish to have—that of being a criminal. This attempt to evade a fate meant he had to be active in reflecting on and acting towards an alternative. He also had to use his relationships (particularly with Mr Warren) to help him achieve this.

Ryan's conflict with Mr Johnson (see page 123) seemed to be about who controlled his ability to act within the woodwork room. He didn't like to have others complete his tasks for him—he preferred to do them himself. However, Ryan seemed unable to act with the preservation of a working relationship with Mr Johnson in mind. By swearing at him, he regularly destroyed the possibility of Mr Johnson helping him. Ryan was unable to contain his annoyance and reflect: 'This is what I want in woodwork, which I like. How can I get it?' After working with me, he was able to do this somewhat, by changing his stance with the teachers. Nevertheless, throughout my contact with Ryan he seemed often surprised by the changes he had wrought, which leads me to wonder how much reflective capacity Ryan had, or simply wasn't telling me about. The changes he made with teachers seemed widespread, across classes. However, without a self-evident capacity for reflection, one wonders how a boy might be able to maintain such changes, particularly after the recognition that goes with any therapeutic contact finishes.

With Charles (see Chapter 6), we have an example of a mother and father engaging with their son in order to assist him to increase his already developing reflective capacity. His example shows that these capacities are not guaranteed—Charles could have remained caught up in a sullen and angry relationship with women for much of his life, and might revert back to this again. There are no guarantees. However, by having ongoing conversations with their son about his conflicts and difficulties, Charles's parents increase their son's chances of emerging from adolescence in a good position for a fulfilling life. This was done by increasing his reflectiveness about his relationships, allowing his agency to emerge on his terms ('out-snobbing') and through discussions where he discovered the importance of his relationships.

These three variables—of relationships, independence of action and reflectiveness—are not increased by parental demands of 'Think about others!', 'You've got to decide what you want to do!' and 'Think before you act!', respectively. One of the important points that I have tried to make through the case studies in this book is that these capacities emerge from a detailed, individual attention and discussion between an adult and an adolescent boy. It is a joint venture that always requires the (at least tacit) cooperation of the boy. The changes I have discussed in Part II cannot be summed up by simple commandments. Rather they are wrought within an on-going, free-ranging discourse, where the adolescent leads at some moments, and the adult leads at others.

Showing As Well As Telling

When parents are dragged into yet another argument with their son, they often forget that sons see their parents doing things as well as listening to their words. This is a crucial distinction to draw. There is a difference between setting limits for a child or adolescent and helping them gain a genuine, internalised respect for an internal set of ethics. None of the techniques outlined in this section will have much chance of succeeding if parents and other adults fail to show as well as tell. In addition, success with boys such as John or Charles may well occur even if none of the techniques in Part II are used, and instead the boy is shown, rather than simply told. I'll explain.

Parents often set limits because it is convenient for them. If I tell my child that he has to be in bed by 8.30 p.m. on school nights, but then allow him to stay up with me some evenings because I am lonely and want someone to keep me company, this sends a message to him. The message is that I am not bound by the same rules as he is, and I can change my mind about rules in accordance with my preferences. Similarly, if I tell my son that he shouldn't hit people, but then hit him when he does something wrong, or become involved in a physical brawl with a neighbour, I am showing him that the rules I enforce don't apply to me and I can change them according to the situation or my wishes. I accept no real limit to my own wishes and desires: I am above the law.

I once knew a school deputy principal who had a particular method of dealing with angry and aggressive boys. He would yell and rage at them as they came into his office, call them stupid and generally be abusive. He told me he was trying to put the boys in their place, subjecting them to some good old-fashioned discipline so they could see some sense. A similar method was adopted by those at the political meeting where the members of the meeting advocated showing a 'bunch of fives' to violent boys.

This approach probably had merit in suppressing some boys' bad behaviour out of fear of facing the deputy principal. I also had the opportunity to hear the boys' views of this teacher and his methods.

Almost universally, boys disliked and resented him and made plans amongst themselves for revenge. Various schemes such as letting down his car tyres and other petty acts of vandalism were discussed. The deputy principal, of course, let it be known that he was not in his job to make friends with the boys. The problem here is that the boys treated in this manner wished to try to place themselves above the law, as the deputy principal seemed to do. For the deputy principal, any method was reasonable to stop boys from being aggressive, but by the teacher acting as if he was above the law, so the boys who were subjected to his rages hoped for or sought a similar position.

This is precisely the problem—of regarding themselves as above the law—that led both John and Alan to act as they pleased. In the moments of their aggressive acts, they considered themselves above the law, or the law or rules to be irrelevant.

If I make as many exceptions to the rule as I like, then I am telling my son that I am not bound by rules. However, if I am really to show my son that there is a rule of law which must be respected, then I am bound by my rules and promises just as much as my son is. Otherwise, the simple progression for the son is to wish somehow to overthrow his parent and dethrone him, thus becoming the one who does exactly as he likes. It is a process that I pay careful attention to in the groups that I run at schools. Within the groups, I try to ensure that the same rule applies to all the members in the group, including me. It then becomes a matter of boys working out how to find their own ways to keep the rules, as they apply to everyone. *There is little possibility of a boy finding a way to keep a law that his own parent does not respect.*

I happen to know that this was probably the difficulty in Alan's case. Though he had a strict father, he had also told me that his father had been convicted for some violent offences. Also, when Alan had been aggressive at home, he had been routinely assaulted by his father as punishment. Alan said, somewhat proudly, that his father had 'bashed' one of the teachers at the school Alan attended when his father and the teacher were teenagers and they had had a disagreement. It seemed that although Alan paid spoken respect to the rules in front of the deputy principal, he also secretly aspired to his father's position: to be the one who could tell others to keep the rules that did not apply to him.

Our relation to rules and the law is complex and evolving. Many parents struggle to keep their children accepting rules that to the individual often seem to contain elements of unfairness. Even in wider society, the actual enforcement of the law seems to rest on a certain arbitrariness and brutality. However, if those people (parents, teachers, youth workers) responsible for deciding and keeping limits for adolescents themselves appear untrustworthy, the less inclined an adolescent will be to accept a limitation to his 'doing what he likes'. This is why it is important for parents not only to tell, but to show that they have a respect for the rules they impose. One can expect parents to fail regularly at doing what they say. However, if a child–adolescent perceives that his parents are attempting to preserve a set of rules or law, then it is likely to result in a greater respect for rules and laws than if the parent continually contravenes his or her own edicts.

Knowing What a Boy Wants

I have stressed several times the importance of knowing about an adolescent's likes and dislikes. It may not be a particularly easy or simple thing to do, but necessary if an adult is to help a young person. There are at least two broad methods. First, from his likes and dislikes, it may be possible to draw out of a young person what he or she might wish to do. This might not be a specific job, or a set of duties, but perhaps a general field, or a generalised desire to go further: finish Year 10, go to the end of school and think about university, do some study at TAFE in computers, carpentry, be involved in the entertainment industry, retail ... these are all wishes that adolescent males have expressed to me at various times. A second method is to notice what an adolescent likes doing, what his aptitudes are, but can't or won't say, and raise this for discussion. Either way, it is important to ground such a wish in the young person's own experience, and remember that wishes for the future are often the product of a back and forth between an adult and a young person over a period of time, often months and years.

Such a 'wish-to-be' is vital on the young person's part, because otherwise there is nothing to lose (as in the case of Greg, page 66). There is no reason to do the work, or exercise restraint from instant gratification. Knowing about this 'wish-to-be' gives the adult something to hold in his or her mind as a reason why a young person would set limits to their anger and wish-fulfilment. Knowledge of the 'wish-to-be' allows the adult to gradually refine and develop the 'wish-to-be' in conversation with adolescents over time. With any boy I have worked with, I have attempted to help him establish this, which always involves talking about the 'wish-to-be'. Without a 'wish-to-be' there are no reasons why a boy would like to work to make any changes. As I discussed in the last chapter, part of the task here is to help a boy see a 'crisis of possibility'. Anger and aggression will not, in the end, get him what he wants.

It does happen that over time a young person can appear to find nothing he wishes or wants to be. All of his starts are false starts, everything becomes too difficult, or not to his liking. This may be a time when it is necessary to seek further help from a professional. Information and principles to help find a relevant professional can be found in the Appendix at the end of this book.

Constant Presence Rather Than Intermittent

Be aware that even though an adolescent boy is reaching towards adulthood, he may still be sensitive to changes in the household. In particular, changes in the availability of parents—both in terms of their physical and mental presences—should be explained. There are many reasons why parents cannot be as available as they may wish to be for their children. Some are unavoidable: tiredness, stress, worrying about other things, parental conflict and problems within the wider family structure. Others, such as use of alcohol and drugs, as well as a parent who cannot physically be there because of the demands of work, can be difficult to change. Such factors mean that a parent can lose touch with his or her children, and problems of conflict can develop without a parent feeling he or she was ever part of the problem.

The alternative, without the presence of an adult encouraging talk, is a descent into a *Lord of the Flies* situation, where the children of the house squabble over what they perceive as scarce commodities. This is despite the fact that in the house there may be plenty of material commodities—an abundance of playthings, food, entertainment and other diversions. Such was the problem in the case of Tania's family: she became aware that she had been spending less time with her children and wondered if this was a factor in their fighting.

Parenting requires an ever-constant presence, which for many parents is at times exhausting and draining. Breaks or interruptions in this presence may mean that effects will be shown by the children. Remember that adolescents still show child-like aspects of their behaviour, and they still tend to *do* things to express how they feel rather than *say* things. A child will probably feel a parent's presence to a greater degree if it is clear that the parent is thinking about the child and discussing his or her thoughts when they are together. This doesn't necessarily require a lot of time.

Listen To and Notice Your Son

Much of what is outlined in this book requires a parent to know his or her son, a teacher to know his or her student: what he does, and what his likes and dislikes are. Knowing this can be some help in assisting a boy. It is to be noted that this is something that neither of David's parents (see page 38) seemed to be able to do. David's mother was so captured by her father's prohibition of nursing as a career for her that she could not listen to her own son's request for guidance, or use what she knew about her son to guide him. Similarly, David's father was too caught up in his fantasies about what he wanted for his son to notice what his son wanted to do, as shown in his subject choices at school, for example. In contrast, Peter and Tania showed a detailed attention to Charles's wishes and wants, particularly in regard to relationships, and allowed this to emerge in discussion.

The Problem of Lecturing

This discussion of talking to your son raises the issue of lecturing. Many parents spend time lecturing their teenagers. Clichés can abound in the lectures parents give their aggressive and angry sons, who are told to 'take responsibility', to 'learn to control your anger', and the like. There is a problem in the plea of 'taking responsibility'. Taken literally, this may be asking a boy to make a *response* that he does not have the *ability* to do. I commonly hear, 'He needs to take responsibility for how he feels'. This statement means little if the boy feels that anger and aggression are the only responses he has the ability to make. Many parents believe that simply talking to one's son will result in a change, but actually it is the manner of talking, a talking which is *aimed at helping a teenager listen to himself*, that is helping his 'I' listen to his 'myself'. Most lectures from parents set out to demonstrate that the son is wrong about himself. Therefore, lecturing a son really only results in either a greater defensiveness or in the end a greater self-punishment. A lecture usually tends to take the parent's world view into account and not the boy's. If there is something the boy is doing that cannot be tolerated, then it should be forbidden, and strongly. It is far preferable than attempting to give him a lecture in accordance with the adult's world view.

What Adults Can Do

This appeared to be what happened in Alan's case, in the repeated lecture from the school's deputy principal. The teacher, intent on laying down the rule of law for the boy, cannot and does not investigate the world view behind Alan's actions. This leaves Alan with little room to find a way of reconciling his feelings of persecution with the school's expectations. All he hears is the school's expectations—which are important in telling him where the limit is. However, telling a boy about a limit and his being able to keep the limit are two altogether different things.

Recognising 'Acting Out'

Anger is almost never a simple, honest emotion. Most angry acts are determined by more than one cause. That is, there are other causes beyond the immediate incident that the angered person is responding to. Recall the discussion of the opportunism of anger and aggression in Chapter 1: adults should attempt to recognise when some outburst belongs somewhere else. Being able to do this requires staying 'in touch' with a boy.

This was something Tania and Peter were able to recognise with Charles and Sabina's conflict. Although she wasn't sure, Tania recognised that the conflict might be occurring on two levels, both as a simple fight between the children and also as a reaction to her being less present in the house. She responded on both levels, to the immediate conflict and also to the problem of her presence. Peter took the problem further, although he could not have known this at the start of his discussions with his son. However, he came to understand that his son's anger was not simply about the Xbox, but as it turned out there was yet another factor. Tied up in his conflict with his sister was a conflict about the emergence of his adolescent sexuality. At the start one cannot know the individual and particular nature of what underlies a boy's anger and aggression. It only emerges in discussion.

Recognising Differences

Just as angry boys commonly have little capacity to recognise times when they have acted differently, just as teachers learn to view a boy in a certain way, one of the most powerful restraints that might prevent a boy from acting differently, and recognising that he has acted differently, is the expectation from his parents that he characteristically acts in a certain way.

Commonly, when I run groups for angry and aggressive boys, I also offer groups the following term for the parents of these same boys. I do this because I have found it useful to help parents recognise the changes that a boy has made as a result of working in a therapy group at school. At times, the barriers to parents recognising that their son is doing something differently are as powerful as a boy's. I outlined a method in Chapter 5 to help adults recognise 'exceptional outcomes', when boys act in a manner that could not have been predicted by their problematic ways of acting previously. Adults who understand that one of their difficulties is recognising positives should reread this chapter.

Stopping aggression is an act of containment by the boy. He withstands the tension created by his frustration, an act which often is not visible to others. However, this can be understood if one knows a boy well enough: a difference is not only what a boy does, but what he does not do. An absence is harder to see than a presence. Yet it is precisely these 'absences' that can be life-changing acts.

Affection and Intimacy

The ideas I have been advocating in this book require a substantial amount of time and effort from adults involved with adolescents. They demand an emotional investment in the outcome of a boy's life that perhaps only a parent, relative, or a teacher or youth worker with a long-term relationship with the boy can have. And it may be, for whatever reasons—the adult's own troubled life history, or still being caught up in his or her own adolescent conflicts, or the circumstances of the boy's birth, or that the boy has driven the adult to distraction, or the limitations of time, or the adult's investment in some other area of life such as a career—that the investment to work with a boy is not present.

A reasonable question to ask oneself if there are serious doubts about your capacity to feel connected to an adolescent (and what parent or adult doesn't have these doubts from time to time?) is: 'What is (or was) my relationship like with my own parents?' Now it is not inevitable that one repeat one's own childhood with one's children. However, if there has been a parental relationship that the parent of an adolescent still finds very troubling, to the point where it is interfering with his or her capacity to parent, or act as a parent-like figure, then this may be a point where the parent should find professional help of his or her own. A parent taking the effort to speak about and understand his or her own difficulties may be the best gift they can give their child.

If an adult does not feel able to invest the time and attention needed, it is probably best that the adult refrain from intervening, rather than moving closer and then having to give up, in a repetitive cycle that will most likely only deepen an adolescent's sense of despair about relationships.

It is a dilemma faced by many parents of children from separated families. One parent has started a new family elsewhere, and that parent's investments are with the new family, not the old one. There are limits to what can be done in such situations. The crucial factors are constancy of involvement over a period of time, a certain responsiveness to the reasonable demands of an adolescent (that is, an ability to listen to the adolescent), and an adult always doing what he says he will. Maintaining a relationship with an adolescent does not necessarily require an extraordinary amount of time, but it does require dependability and being able to inconvenience oneself at crucial times.

In addition, as attested by the grief-stricken group of boys discussed in Chapter 2, love is a start, but it is not enough. Indeed, adults also need a sense of the three aspects of capacity for reflection, a belief in the importance of relationships and a sense that they can bring about change if they are to be able to help an angry adolescent. These capacities brought to bear on parenting an adolescent are more important than the sheer amount of time or money spent on a child.

Rules and Limits

Parents often get caught in the vexed issues of rules and attempting to make their adolescent sons keep them. Endless fights can ensue about rules, whether they are about what an adolescent cannot do (that is, setting limits on his freedoms) or about what he must do (that is, responsibilities around the house). One of the difficulties here is that there are no inviolable rules to getting the balance right, between allowing an adolescent to manage himself on the one hand and giving him firm guidance on what is not allowed or what is expected on the other.

The overall aim is twofold. First, to ensure that an adolescent makes it through adolescence without doing too much damage to his long-term prospects. With this in mind, it is reasonable that parents set clear boundaries that mean the adolescent remains safe, carries through on some future-building endeavour such as study, training or work, and doesn't break any major laws.

However, a second, just as important aim for an adolescent is to learn to limit himself, to set his own rules and be able to apply these rules flexibly and appropriately. The golden rule of rules is: *how can adolescents find their own freedom inside the rules?* This is not something that is learnt through parents keeping a relentless, rigid guard up on rules. This is something an adolescent learns through

What Adults Can Do

discussions around and about rules, through seeing how a parent reasons and by talking with them about the whys and wherefores of rules. This second aspect of rules is achieved more through showing an adolescent rather than telling.

Here are some important points to keep in mind about rules in adolescence.

- Too many rules do not leave an adolescent room to begin to negotiate and set rules himself. As adolescence progresses there should be fewer rules, and the rules should be more general in nature.

- Too many rules mean an adolescent will resent the parent who sets the rules, and not own the rules himself. *Too many rules leave no room for the adolescent to take responsibility for his own conduct.* In the end, this is the primary aim of rules, beyond the concerns about security and safety in adolescence.

- Authoritarian setting of rules is unlikely to be effective, if you have not gained a boy's cooperation. Many parents, with the best intentions in mind, create a strict regime of limits without discussing them with the boy, or being able in any realistic way to offer consequences if the limits are broken. The boy often cannot see how it is in his interests to follow such rules.

- A certain degree of negotiation, conflict and arguing about rules is, if not inevitable, perhaps a necessary adjunct to a son developing the responsibilities that go with the gradually increasing freedoms of adolescence. *An ongoing discussion about rules means that rules are working.* The discussion might involve a greater or lesser amount of anger and pushing against the rules. The fact that the discussion is occurring means that a son still values the mutual limit that a parent or teacher has set, but wishes to negotiate about a specific limit. This is a healthy sign of developing independence.

Arguing, quarrelling and negotiating about rules can be tiresome, exasperating, tedious and exhausting—but the alternative is far worse. The alternative generally means that an adolescent acts out his protest about the rules, rather than speaking about them. Such an alternative can be extremely problematic, and may be a sign that a family or son needs further help. Here are some warning signs.

Rebellion

Rather than an adolescent discussing with the parent or teacher his concerns about the rules, he 'acts out' in a wilful attempt to show the adult that he doesn't care about breaking them. To the adult it will appear that the adolescent is breaking the rules simply for the sake of it. That is, because certain things are expected, the adolescent simply acts against them, often to the point of his own destruction. Such a situation can be particularly exasperating and disempowering for a parent. The adult attempts to assert his or her authority in the name of the well-being of the adolescent, but the adolescent seems bent on undermining this authority. The problem—which parents are quite rightly worried about—is the self-destructive nature of an adolescent's actions, which have the capacity to do long-term damage to his future.

In such situations there is always something more to the relationship than the adolescent simply being wilful, although it is clear that child and parent are locked in a power struggle. Beyond the power struggle, the adolescent son is nearly always trying to express something that he has been unwilling or unable to express in words. The real struggle is to help the adolescent put into words what he is currently conveying in actions. I outlined a method in Chapter 5 that enables adults to help adolescent boys put into words what is expressed in actions, and this method is useful for a rebelling adolescent.

It may also be that the power struggle is such that it is impossible to have a constructive discussion with an adolescent. If this is the

What Adults Can Do

case, a boy needs further help. Places to seek further help are discussed in the Appendix.

A Secret Life

An alternative to discussing and disputing rules is that the adolescent develops a 'secret life', which may or may not be one that is self-destructive. I have heard many parents complain that although their son seems to agree to all the rules, they have a certain unease with the ease of his agreement—that he has another, secret, life they know nothing about, but get to hear about once the school or other parents call. Of course, for a pubescent boy to begin to develop a secret life is absolutely normal: there are more and more aspects of an adolescent's own life that he keeps to himself as adolescence progresses. In this type of problem, the adolescent uses his increased independence to break the same rules he agrees to. His parents tend to worry that they have lost touch with their boy—that he does and thinks things that they do not have access to or a connection with. Again, I described in Chapter 5 a process where a parent can begin to keep in touch with a boy's life and start the process of helping him speak about his difficulties. If parents have concerns about the secret life of an adolescent, they can use this method to get back in touch with their boy.

Obedience

If there is no conflict between parents and an adolescent over rules this can be a danger, as it may mean that a boy is failing to develop his own particular take on what he might like to attain his life. It is a problem because the boy may be taking up his parents' view of the world, without the difficulty of finding his own way, genuinely separating.

This is a path Greg (see page 66) could have adopted. He could have simply taken up his family values of stealing and repairing cars, and being somewhat outside the law, resigned to the fact that he would get a criminal record as a rite of passage. He did not want this. It is remains somewhat of a mystery as to why this was the case but my guess would be that his powers of reflection on his circumstance helped him. He was able to see the implication of his position in his family.

Commonly, in cases where an adolescent does not protest over rules, his protest emerges in another way, such as sadness or an attack on himself. I saw a young teenage boy named Anthony who as a child had been very overweight, as were both his parents. The boy bore many other symptoms of his parents: social anxiety, depression and the like. He had never caused his mother any difficulties at home and had regularly attended church meetings and domestic violence support meetings with her, although she had been separated from his father and without a partner since Anthony was two years old. Anthony had been shuffled back and forth between mother and father every six months. The most prominent of Anthony's symptoms when he came to see me was anorexia: he had not eaten properly for a year. Though I am not going into the details of this case, it was clear that his refusal to eat was a silent protest against his suffocation by his mother.

Finally, the boy who is endlessly obedient can also store up hurts and wrongs until he cannot stand his inner tension any more and explodes incomprehensibly at some minor slight. Such boys often require help from an adult, who can help him see the problem of ignoring anger that might be felt, how he should not push away another slight. It is necessary for a parent to take the boy's viewpoint and look out for him if this occurs. In reality, the problem is only brought to the fore over time, when a boy reacts angrily to seemingly insignificant slights. Then one must review the lead-up to the outburst, to see what else may have contributed to it (see also pages 10–11, where I discuss the tendency for anger to be displaced away from its cause).

Parents Working Together

It is a matter of course that the parents of a boy will have different approaches to being with their child. However, parents can talk about what is happening in the family and adjust their parenting accordingly. I have commonly worked with more or less extreme cases where (often separated) parents have different expectations.

> Graham, a 12-year-old boy, spent every second weekend with his father, and the remainder of the time with his mother. His mother worked hard at setting limits: on bedtime, TV-watching, sweet foods, take-away and the like. However, his father had the opposite approach. Graham regularly came home from his father's house saying it had been a party and became very angry when his mother attempted to enforce the rules of her house. She became an overbearing suffocator of Graham's freedoms. This led to many interminable angry scenes between son and mother.

The point is not about where the rules actually are, but the difference between the rules of the mother and the father. Graham started to aspire to the life of seeming luxury that his unemployed father enjoyed, where he did not have to submit to any rules and could lounge most of the day watching TV and playing the Playstation. He grew to hate the restrictions and regime in the house of his working mother.

All this came not from what Graham was told by his father, but from what he saw as the difference between his parents. Some agreement on common rules is important in these situations, not because of the rules themselves but because of the problems such dramatic inconsistencies create.

Conflict between parents is almost inevitable, but is at its most damaging when the child is either consciously or unconsciously drawn into any conflict. This happens most often when parents—those who are together as well as those who are separated—are unable to speak openly together about their differences.

Forbidding

The reasons for a rule have been explained, the son is still begging and pleading desperately, and the parent has thought about the issue and is convinced it is definitely not in the adolescent's interest to be allowed to go to a party, go away with a friend and his family, or travel to a distant part of town with another friend.

And there it has to stop. One of the difficulties about parenting an adolescent is that a parent decides what is in the adolescent's interest, even though the adolescent seems to have many adult-like abilities, not least of which is the capacity to reason and argue. In the end, the adolescent obeys the parent, because the parent is the adolescent's parent, and this is what limits the adolescent's risk-taking and endless pursuit of enjoyment. For this reason, a parent is not a friend in the ordinary sense of the word, although there may be moments in adolescence where the relationship is friendship-like.

The difference between a parent and a friend is that a parent holds in mind what is in his or her son's best interest. To a friend, it matters less what a boy does: either he wants to or he doesn't.

The function of forbidding, as I have discussed above, has vital formative influences on an adolescent that should not be under-estimated. In Chapter 3 I argued that it can be seen as a function of a father, even if the prohibition comes from the mother herself. In the current context of single-parent families—boys being raised increasingly by single mothers with only part-time or intermittent contact with their fathers, or rivalrous relations with step-fathers who cannot take up the role of saying 'No'—this 'paternal function' seems to be in danger of extinction.

However, the paternal function has an important contribution to make in limiting a boy's enjoyment, his staying inside the rules, taking responsibility for his own actions, and generally limiting the degree to which he is dominated by a paranoid habit of mind. This failure is apparent in the case of Graham that I discussed above. Graham's father failed to limit any of his freedoms; on the contrary, by example he encouraged Graham to take whatever freedoms he wished. Graham then found recurrent reasons to blame his mother for all of the restrictions she caused and problems he had. She came to be blamed for all his difficulties—a tendency familiar from other cases earlier in the book, and one which did not bode well for the remainder of Graham's adolescence. Graham was not separating from his mother, only shifting his relationship with her from love to hate.

The point is that prohibition is protective, not just against the straightforward dangers that justify the prohibition. It is also protective against the development of a paranoid, other-blaming tendency to anger and aggression.

The Restructuring of Enjoyment

I have argued on several occasions in this book that parents have to assist adolescents to institute a limit to enjoyment, in order for an adolescent to get want he wants. This is something that happens as a matter of course in many cases, although an implication of the previous section is that with the fall of the paternal function, perhaps anger and aggression are on the rise. However, most people are able to keep the law, and don't have to experience a feeling of 'breaking the rules' in order to feel alive (although many would argue that people transgress in many other ways, behind closed doors in the bedroom, for example). Although the phenomenon of transgression is probably far more widespread than I claim here, I am restricting the discussion to violence and aggression.

In any case, the function of limiting enjoyment is one that needs to be borne in mind. Gradually over months and months this is something that happened in the case of Greg (see page 66). His enjoyment of dope smoking, of hitting whoever he wanted, thinking that the school rules did not apply to him, were gradually restructured by his ideals kept alive by his teacher and an ongoing dialogue with me. It enabled him to exchange 'I'll do whatever I feel like' with 'I want this, and I'm prepared to work towards it'. Greg was eventually able to solve the puzzle of 'How can I work to get what I want, without causing problems that cross the law?' This happened through the reprioritising of what he wanted over what he could enjoy.

Doubt Revisited

It is not unusual for adolescents to appear certain of their futures, of 'What I'm going to do', presented in a rather grandiose way. Adolescence is a time of high ideals and plans to match. The world is the problem and it had better get out of the way! As I discussed in Chapter 4, add chronic anger, a paranoid habit of mind and aggression to this picture and it changes somewhat. High ideals turn into nasty, attacking certainties which serve as excuses to attack, demean and punish others. They often allow the aggressive boy to set himself above his contemporaries and be free from the rules that others have to follow.

When I have written about the importance of replacing the certainty of angry adolescents with doubt, I do not mean dimming the ideals of adolescence, however unrealistic they may be. Ideals serve an important developmental function, a goal, a purpose upon which to reflect and make sense of the world and its goings on.

Rather, the creation of doubt serves the function of creating questions in the face of aggressive certainties. These questions must be the right questions, not just any questions. Any notion or act which potentially damages a boy's relationships with those around him, where he hides his part in the drama of his life, diminishes or gives up his ability to act independently towards his own aims, or retreats from the reflective work that might uncover painful truths, is an area that is ripe for questioning. The function of doubt is to create more questions, and open new areas of thought and discussion, just as Peter did with Charles.

Too Much Talk

There are limits to all this talk. In general, adolescents become bored and distracted with too much detail. It is best to restrict things to broad brushstrokes and let adolescents fill in the details in their own way. Notice in Chapter 6 that Peter and Tania did not speak a huge volume of words to their children. They had dialogues with them, making short interventions where necessary. They then let Charles fill in the gaps.

In particularly painful areas, places where doubt does indeed dominate (although it may be covered by a certainty), boys' ideas and thoughts about themselves, the story they tell about themselves, may fall apart. A boy may feel he is starting to disintegrate under the weight of words and uncertainties, and this is a place where conflict can easily begin, and the dialogue falls victim to the boy's anger and paranoia. Indeed, he may find even starting to venture towards these places too threatening. I gave a description of one such encounter with Daniel (see page 63) where our discussions got to the point where he suddenly curled into a ball, clamped his hands over his ears and screamed repetitively, 'I'm not listening to you any more! I'm not listening to you any more!'

There can be too much talk, talk which angry adolescents find destructive, and at these times it is best to take a break. It is possible to read the signs prior to the point of 'too much'. Don't force a boy to talk about something he doesn't want to. Allow a boy to lead, don't push him around enquiring into areas where he may not want to go. Read the signs of reluctance that might be manifest in his body, in his tone of voice, but which he might not be able to utter in speech.

8
Intervening with the School

Wayne was a boy who was causing multiple difficulties at school. Over the short time I worked with him he locked a female teacher in a small storage room for an hour, taunting her through the window. He also destroyed the plumbing in the boys' toilets, swore at teachers and got into several fights. However, Wayne was an intelligent, insightful, articulate, tall and handsome boy. He also came, by the reports of the school, from a religious, law-abiding family whose parents took a keen interest in their son. It did not seem to add up that this teenager could do such destructive things.

When I met Wayne he expressed doubt that much could be done to help with his problems. 'I just get this jumpiness inside of me and I can't stop myself from doing something about it. In some ways I don't mind it because … well, people say I talk too much … but I like talking … but I don't mind being frustrated sometimes because it tells me I have to do something, even though it gets me into trouble. I think I just go too far. I can't stop. They tried to medicate me for a while, but I stopped taking it because it was like living under a wet blanket. They told me I'm on my last chance at school, and so I decided to start taking my medication again because it does stop me getting into trouble. I go to the office every recess and lunch to get it, because otherwise I forget.'

Wayne also told me he'd been sent to many psychiatrists and psychologists and didn't see how anything new could come of my involvement. Even though I had found him likeable, easy to work with and talk to, I honoured his doubt and told him that if he felt he needed my help in the future, he could contact me. As I was about to leave, he suddenly said, 'OK—I'll meet with you on one condition, that you don't tell me to stop talking. I hate when you counsellors tell me to stop talking … that's how I get my frustration out. And I want us to have a try out first, to see how it goes.' I told him that when he was meeting with me, he could say whatever he liked.

After meeting Wayne I spoke to the deputy principal about him, who informed me that he had quite a lot of difficulty dealing with the problems Wayne caused at school. The teacher felt that this was less to do with Wayne and more to do with the reception he received from the family. Each time he attempted to raise Wayne's problems in meetings with the family, in private or within parent–teacher interviews, the parents immediately sided with their son and would not allow the school to discipline Wayne in any way. The deputy told me Wayne would sit in the interview half-smiling, with his arms crossed, not saying anything, while the deputy principal and the parents battled over whether Wayne was responsible for his actions. For example, when the deputy principal spoke to the parents regarding Wayne locking the teacher in the storeroom, the parents asked what the teacher was doing in the storeroom and suggested that perhaps she should not have been there.

Now, although Wayne's parents apparently felt they were doing the best by their son, by supporting him against the punishments meted out by the school, in fact they were not doing him any favours. They were making it very difficult for their son to 'fit in' with the normal limits of school. By always siding with the boy against the deputy principal, in front of the deputy principal, they were giving Wayne 'a way out' from school discipline. Wayne began to look at suspensions as holidays. In the end, after a long series of suspensions and interviews similar to the one the deputy principal described, the school had little choice but to expel Wayne. An intelligent boy, his studies were badly affected.

His story has a happier ending, in that on expulsion from his third school, he found work with a builder who took him under his wing. The builder, a fellow a dozen years older than Wayne, accepted Wayne into his family, taking him away on holidays and asking Wayne to assist with babysitting and the preparation of family meals. The builder was able to inculcate into Wayne the importance of work and responsibility while having enjoyment and pleasure at other times.

It is probable that Wayne was able to make use of this opportunity because of his ability to reflect on his relationships. In his initial interview with me he seemed to be demanding that someone listen to him, help him sort things out. In his manner of speaking he seemed always to be grasping for something, unable to reach it. He was also very particular about what he was agreeing to with me, which can be taken as a good sign. He was elastic and muscular in the way he thought about relationships; he certainly wasn't passively accepting what was happening to him. This is probably what made him so difficult for the school. He never accepted rules for their own sake, but made forceful use of his own reasons as to why he should be an exception to the rule—which unfortunately often led to his use of aggression. It was this same quality of 'arguing for being an exception' that also made him so likeable.

Intervening with the School

Wayne's example has shades of the problem of mother and father roles I discussed in Chapter 3. It seems his parents loved him and wanted the best for him. However, just as with rules, love is not enough. Both parents were acting in the position of mother, supporting their son unconditionally in front of the principal. No one was prepared to support the school and say, 'Wayne, that is enough. There are certain things expected of you in school and you have to keep the rules.'

In some ways this position is understandable. I can sympathise with Wayne's parents. It is true that some principals do have a fairly ruthless attitude with difficult adolescents. I have been to many deputy principal–parent interviews that do not go well because the parents themselves have a problem with their son having to fit in with the rules of the school. Speculatively, Wayne's parents might well have been reacting to experiences from their own upbringings, which they were attempting to correct in their child.

I recall one extreme case, where a father came to an interview to discuss his child's misbehaviour with the same deputy principal who had expelled him from the same local school many years earlier. The interview did not go well. The father found it difficult to step into the role of a parent in front of the deputy principal. The school's accusations against his child seem to return him to the same position of being persecuted that he had felt as a teenager. He proceeded to defend his child against all of the school's accusations. This robbed his child of the chance to take responsibility for what he had done. As in Wayne's case, the child was eventually expelled.

For Wayne, the behaviour of the parents had not resulted in an entirely negative outcome. Wayne was good with words, likeable, and somehow able to get you on his side before you even knew it. The downside was his utter petulance and dangerous and destructive recklessness if he failed in his attempts to get what he wanted.

School is one of the first tests of whether a boy is able to adapt to the environment immediately outside the family. Wayne's parents unwittingly made sure that he failed the test by giving him the illusion that they were able to shelter him from having to fit in with the demands and restrictions of daily life. How a boy goes at school is an important measure of his ability to cope with mainstream society. Schools are simply a reflection of the culture they exist within and are not perfect but a parent cannot shelter their child from the imperfection of the wider world forever. An important task of adolescence is that a boy should cope with the increased self-reliance demanded in secondary schools.

There was no rule worth keeping for Wayne's parents except to shelter their son from threatening forces outside the family. The case illustrates how the interface between school and family is a crucial one. How parents negotiate this interface on behalf of their son can have an important impact on the degree to which school functions as a means of separation from the family, a trajectory which is essential to an adolescent being ready to assume adult responsibilities. Wayne's parents' undercutting of the school's attempts to enforce the rules seemed to give him the message that he didn't have to keep the rules like anyone else. It meant that school could not perform the important function of aiding the transition between child and adult life. Wayne was caught in the position of a child whose parents continued to shelter him from the adult world. In a way, Wayne's parents were sheltering him from an encounter with the giant hands of the pedestrian crossing (see pages 31–4). The parents' acts rendered the hands invisible, and thus Wayne had no means of discovering his own relationship with the rules.

In this chapter, I will discuss some approaches that parents can take when problems emerge at school. Generally, the outcome of such problems is improved if parents actively seek to investigate the problem both with the son and with the school. Parents can sort through what they hear, then in discussion with each other and their son arrive at a conclusion, perhaps a plan for action. Later in this chapter I also outline ideas that parents and teachers can use to alter the culture of a school if this is feasible.

Investigating the Problem: Approaching the Adolescent

Generally, as part of the process of 'staying in touch' with a boy, parents have discussions with him about how things are going at school. One would expect a boy to bring up problems such as failed test results, missed assignments, incidents at school, detentions and suspensions. If this doesn't happen or the news of a suspension is a complete surprise (and normally in the case of suspensions a parent hears first from the school), it may be important to spend more time discussing how things are going at school, for there probably is a problem.

Express disappointment if you disapprove of your son's behaviour, but also be sure to understand his point of view. You may be the only person who does. It will not be effective to isolate a boy completely because this will only increase his sense of being a victim. Try to find out what the problem is from his point of view. There may be particular problems at school such as bullying, certain teachers he does not like, or groups who are trying to isolate him. His anger may be a symptom of these difficulties. It is best if you can work with your son, but to help *him* intervene to fix the problem rather than taking the problem out of his hands. Steps for doing so are outlined in Chapters 5 and 6. As always, think broadly about the problem—could there be underlying reasons for the difficulties at school?

There are exceptions to leaving a son to solve the problem himself. If the problem is one of bullying and you feel that there is a culture of increasing violence at the school, that is a time for a parent to intervene directly with the school. Parents must act to ensure a son's safety.

There is a delicate balancing act between safety and increasing a son's capacity to fend for himself, make decisions for himself, in line with increasing the developing capacities of adolescence. At the other extreme to Wayne's parents are those who never come to school and remain distant from the son's school life.

Investigating the Problem: Approaching the School

In discovering more about the problem, it may be important to approach the school. In doing this, parents may need to be persistent. Schools are busy places. Though many have systems in place for contacting parents when there is a problem, often the reverse—where a parent attempts to contact a staff member at the school—is more difficult.

Despite these difficulties, ask to speak directly with both those responsible in the school (normally the deputy principal) and also the staff member who witnessed the behaviour a boy has been accused of. It is then possible, if necessary, to return to your son and discuss what you have heard.

If there is difficulty speaking to the correct person, whether it is the deputy principal, the boy's year adviser, mentor teacher or specific subject teacher, don't take things personally. Many teachers (perhaps quite rightly) see their main task as one of education, not welfare. If there are difficulties, many parents feel blamed by the school for their son's problems, even in the absence of any evidence that this is the case. Just as a boy must limit his paranoid habit of mind, so must parents.

An important lesson from Wayne's case is that it is in a son's best interest that parents find a way of working with and communicating with the school. A war between a boy's family and the school will not help him find a way of existing comfortably in school. Rather, a battle like this will undermine the demands of the school and generally make the processes of education and maturation for a boy more difficult.

If you are told of a problem concerning your son at school, despite what you hear at school you can still support him. Even though you may have reasons to fully believe the school's account of events, remember that there is a kernel of truth in every act of anger and violence. It is the school's role to set limits on an aggressive boy's behaviour, thus limiting the damage he may cause. It is the parents' (and perhaps an interested teacher's) role to investigate how the incident occurred from the boy's point of view. Steps for investigating and discussing such incidents constructively are outlined in Chapter 5.

Parents Taking Action

There may be several issues to take up both with a school and with an adolescent.

First, be sure to discuss the problem fully with the adolescent. Use the Cycle of Identity (outlined in Chapter 5) to help him understand his part in the problem.

- *Action to description*: What happened? What did he do? What were his reasons?
- *Description to meaning*: What does he think about it now? Did he talk about what happened with any of his classmates? What did they think? Has he talked about what happened with any of his teachers? How does he feel about the punishment that the school has given him?
- *Meaning to performing–meaning*: Assist a boy to come up with ideas to deal with the difficulty in the days and weeks after an aggressive incident. Would he do the same thing again? What are the advantages and disadvantages of this? How are things going with the others who were involved in the conflict? Are things better or worse at school generally? Why is this?

Your son may have given you a broader picture of the incident, one that it may be important to discuss with the school. This may prevent things from getting to the point in a school where a boy feels so weighed down by his reputation that he has to leave (as in the case of John, pages 112–16).

In addition, there may be agreements that can be made with the school, such as being notified when certain things happen so these may be discussed with the boy (although ideally it would be best to be able to rely on a son to tell you himself). Such agreements are important to ensure that generally a parent is involved and is monitoring the situation; the boy should know about any school–parent agreement, so he feels supported by the parent. Asking for general, regular discussions in the months following an incident means that a parent keeps in touch with the ebb and flow of how the school is viewing the boy. Making such attempts to stay involved and in touch with the school will generally weigh in a boy's favour, and a school will usually treat a student with parents who are available this way more positively.

Teachers Taking Action with Aggressive Students

There is a very wide literature on working with or teaching difficult students, and I will not cover it fully here. I will simply attempt to illustrate several key techniques that teachers can use in and around the classroom and playground to help boys with anger problems.

The Importance of Relationships with Teachers

Recall the example of Greg in Chapter 3. He had managed to form an important relationship with a teacher, Mr Warren. The effect of this relationship was that it was able to help Greg do something that he knew was in his best interests, but which he found difficult. This was captured in his statement that Mr Warren 'could teach us, even though we did not want to learn'. Mr Warren had become, for Greg, an alternative father figure, someone to look up to. How did this come about?

One can't make a relationship of admiration and trust just happen. Though it is possible to encourage such a relationship, one cannot make it occur. Perhaps one of the most powerful forces that encourage a boy's development of a positive relationship is the

Intervening with the School

teacher taking time to listen to his point of view. This is more difficult to achieve in a secondary school as opposed to primary school. Many boys entering secondary school find the movements from class to class and the number of different teachers to be quite a shock. Whereas in the past a boy had a teacher who knew his foibles and eccentricities well, it is not always the case in a secondary setting. This is developmentally appropriate for many boys, but those with anger and aggression problems find that secondary teachers are less accommodating than their previous teachers. It makes the process of forging relations with such boys early in secondary school all the more important. However, such relationships often fail to develop, precisely because of the boy's behaviour and this makes early intervention in secondary school (from both teachers and parents) all the more important.

Some points to follow in helping a teacher–student relationship develop are:

- Look for signs that a boy is forming a special attachment to you.

- Choose your target. There may simply be some boys whom you can't connect with. Remember that angry and aggressive boys often repel teachers, and no one can connect with them. Perhaps another teacher, one who knows how to connect with difficult boys, is needed here.

- When there is a disturbance in class caused by the boy, as much as possible try to contain the problem in class, although this may be difficult. Call on the support of other teachers and colleagues if necessary.

- If the boy does cause a problem, don't resile from any consequences (meting out punishment) that are necessary, as if you don't you may send a message to the boy that he is special and somehow above the rules.

- Acknowledge your mistakes if you make some in response to a boy. If you come to know that you have accused him wrongly, discuss this.

- Techniques for discussion, meaning-making and helping the boy think through his actions, outlined in Chapter 5, can be used in moments outside the classroom.

- Follow the same rules you request of the boys (see page 177).

- If you have to send an aggressive boy out of class, follow the steps in helping a boy reflect on anger (see Chapter 6). Don't let misbehaviour go undiscussed once the bell for the end of class comes. This only builds unspoken resentment about what happened. Try to sort it out, to find out from the boy his point of view and reason for doing what he did.

Steve—Managing Difficulties In and Out of Class

About three weeks into first term, Steve, a 14-year-old Year 8 boy, had been teased by two other boys at the start of the class. The teasing was in response to the teacher's questions and was seemingly good-natured. Steve had laughed it off and the teacher assumed that he was okay with the comments. However, during the class, Steve gradually became more and more disruptive, removing chair leg stoppers and throwing them at other class members. When the teacher asked him to stop he became enraged and swore, telling the class they were idiots, and throwing his chair to one side.

The teacher asked Steve to have time out, sitting outside the door. The teacher set the class some work and went out to speak with Steve. The teacher immediately made a guess, and quickly described the teasing and the chain of events leading up to the chair-throwing, asking Steve about his internal reactions

Intervening with the School

to the events. Steve calmed as the teacher spoke, eventually agreeing that talking about anger in the time out had 'brought it down'. An anger work plan was also discussed. First, Steve agreed to let the teacher know if incidents in class made him angry. Second, if he couldn't do this, Steve could have a time out and the teacher would help him to talk about anger in future time outs, in the event of overwhelming anger in the class.

The teacher also said that while he knew Steve was upset, he could not allow swearing in his class; Steve agreed not to swear in the future. Steve returned to the class on the condition that the teacher assisted him to ask the class not to insult him. Steve also decided he would replace the stoppers on the chairs, thus 'repairing' the damage he had caused.

On return to class, Steve remained quiet and focused. At the end of the lesson, the teacher spoke with Steve before he left, asking how he had been able to stay quiet. Steve replied it was because he felt the teacher had not just blamed him, but seen things from his point of view. The teacher made a note of this for future interventions and problems. Steve also asked if he could talk to him if there were problems in the future.

Many teachers simply will not have the capacity to make time like this for Steve, particularly in the face of an unruly class. If such discussion cannot happen during the class, the bell between classes may be a useful time to carry out such work. The salient points here are:

- Rather than moving straight to discussion of the behaviour, the teacher acknowledged Steve's internal experience.
- The teacher asked Steve for an ideal ('let me know when you are angry') and also a fallback ('have a time out'), knowing that Steve might have a lot of difficulty letting the teacher know about his anger. He might not be able to let himself know about it just yet.

Such a two-fold request meant the teacher and Steve had something to work towards, as well as a strategy for handling the problem in the meantime when the ideal, inevitably, was not reached. This plan, of course, should be rediscussed and modified in future time outs.

- It was only after acknowledging Steve's emotions that the teacher moved to the problem of his behaviour. It is a necessary first step with chronically angry boys—it does not need to take much time, but involves thinking about the problem from the boy's point of view.
- The teacher did not abandon Steve to enact his own solutions. He offered Steve help to put them in place.

Taking Action: Helping a Student Teach the Teacher

Angry and aggressive boys often complain that they are being picked on for things they haven't done, and are singled out by teachers when something goes wrong in the class. Often the boy's complaint may be based in fact. Much research has shown that those who have contact with an angry and aggressive boy tend to treat him with the same suspicion that he treats others. However, the complaint of the boy seldom seems to help him find a way out of being blamed. Rather, his victim-hood pushes him to do things that confirm the teacher's view of him. Angry boys need help to get out of this cycle. A boy is ready to be helped if the following things have occurred:

- He has complained repeatedly about being blamed for things he didn't do.
- He has agreed that he doesn't like being 'picked on' by teachers. (He may also agree that he is sick of being angry with teachers and teachers being angry with him.)

- He has agreed to try something different to stop being blamed.

The following are some steps that may used to help an aggressive boy out of this cycle of blame.

1. **Figure out with the boy what it is he is doing** to annoy the teacher, or to cause a problem. For example:

- Ask the boy to think about his interaction with a teacher from the teacher's point of view. The teacher, in charge of thirty students in a busy classroom, wants to stamp out any misbehaviour as quickly as it starts. What is that the boy is doing that makes it hard for the teacher?

- If the boy is not sure what he is doing wrong, encourage him to approach the teacher at the start or end of a period and ask. If the boy is not confident enough to do this, then ask him to suggest someone who could help him ask the teacher.

2. **Try to figure out what others do** that might cause the problem. Ask the boy:

- Is there something the teacher does that he wishes the teacher would change? If so, would the boy talk to the teacher about it?

- Are there other things happening in the class the boy doesn't like? For example, teasing (see the example of Steve, above)?

- If the problem is nothing to do with the teacher or classmates, can the boy identify when the problem is about to arise? For example:
  - if he finds the work boring, is there some way the teacher could make it interesting?
  - if the work isn't understood, would the boy ask the teacher for help?
  - if the boy is scared of 'appearing dumb', would he ask the teacher for help in private?

Implementing a Plan for Improving School Behaviour

- Parents should help a boy to stop doing the things that annoy the teacher (see above).

- *Don't* expect a teacher to change his or her attitude to a boy overnight. It may take as long as two months before you see any behaviour change from the teacher's side. Remember, a boy is going to have to 'teach the teacher' about the real version of himself, who wants to do well and is not a troublemaker.

- *Prepare* the boy for the fact that the teacher will continue to blame him for things he no longer does, but once did. The teacher is using a boy's reputation, not 'the real boy'.

- Coach a boy: 'If you are accused wrongly by a teacher then *respond calmly*'. Many teachers take it as an admission of guilt when a student responds angrily. Tell the boy to say gently, firmly and respectfully, 'I didn't do that, Sir/Mrs/Miss.'

Further Points

- Don't let a boy get away with blaming the teacher. Simply express sympathy with how tough it is in a certain class he has difficulty with, but don't go along with 'Mr Smith is a bastard towards me'. This allows an angry boy to continue with his habit of blaming others.

- A boy's reputation, reflected back to him by others, may be a major barrier to success here. Teachers and peers expect a boy to be aggressive and angry if he has been so extensively in the past. This is where a boy may need help when he is not instantly rewarded for his change in attitude, which often results in a deepening of his despair: 'I tried to change, but it didn't make any difference'. In these situations, there needs to be someone—a teacher, parent, counsellor or deputy principal—who can recognise the change in the boy's attitude, and actions, in the absence of immediate results.

Taking Action: If an Adolescent Has Fallen In with the 'Wrong Crowd'

I discussed in Chapter 4 the characteristics of the adolescent group, and how adolescent membership of peer groups is enormously important for the development of an adult self outside the family of origin. I described how adolescents used membership of groups to extend, enhance or experiment with aspects of themselves. It is in the context of such groups that an adolescent slowly gathers, modifies or extends a sense of 'Who I wish to be.'

Conversely, adolescent groups have enormous potential to lead a boy into paths where he diminishes or gives up his own ideas, goals and wishes. This phenomenon of effacing oneself for the membership of a group is particularly pronounced in aggressive and violent youth gangs, and can delay, derail or completely destroy the process of separation in adolescence. There is much evidence that boys who feel marginalised at school use a group of similarly marginalised boys to assuage the negative feelings that result from rejection from the mainstream. These boys regularly feel as if they have right on their side when they engage in aggressive, violent and vengeful acts.

It is thus of concern if a parent sees his or her son 'falling in' with the wrong crowd at school. A parent must consider thoughtfully whether a boy is simply going outside the normative strictures of his family, or whether he is being part of something that risks his long-term prospects, in psychological, legal and developmental terms.

What Parents Should Do
If you are worried about a boy's acquaintances, or if your son is a member of a gang that is clearly having a negative effect on him, it may be best to be forceful and intervene to remove him from the

influence of anti-social peers. One of the strongest predictors of negative outcomes in maturity is allegiance with anti-social peers but it is unclear whether this is a result of boys being rejected and banding together, or whether the group itself causes the negative outcomes.

However, parents should first, before taking strong action:

- Investigate the nature of a boy's friendships.

- Watch for changes in a boy's attitudes and behaviour. If there is a sudden shift that seems completely at odds with opinions he held previously, this might be a cause for concern.

- Discuss the history of ideas that have emerged suddenly. Why does he think what he thinks? How justifiable is the set of ideas?

- Discuss any changes in attitude with the boy. How fixed do they seem?

- Remember that groups are the primary mode of social expression in adolescence. They are an important means for an adolescent to 'find his feet' in his expanding social world. Groups allow boys to find a means of 'keeping the law', a means that they discover themselves and is not imposed upon them. A group can teach an adolescent to preserve a set of friendships and relationships that mean he must act in a certain way. Talk about the comings and goings of a boy's friendships with him.

- Many parents misunderstand this function of peers and feel rejected by their adolescent when he starts to value his friendships more than his familial relationships. Accept a boy's membership of a group as part of the normal process of things if it does not seem to be having a negative effect.

- Look for expression of power relations. Don't allow a boy to timidly or unintelligently accept his 'place' in a group. Turn power

Intervening with the School

relations you hear your son describe into communications by talking about them (use the Cycle of Identity in Chapter 5).

- Encourage questions, reflection and the discussion of multiple perspectives as an antidote to the single, violence-promoting viewpoint of the aggressive adolescent group.
- Don't try to enforce your views on a boy. This is a similar power relation as occurs in the group, and will likely result in a power struggle for intellectual supremacy.
- Think about the meaning of a boy suddenly becoming part of a violent peer group. Is he taking refuge from something? If so what? Could this be an unconscious protest? If so, against what? Think more broadly about the boy's circumstances and discuss these with him.
- Has your son stopped caring? If so, why?
- Don't be backward in making contact with other boys' parents and find out what sorts of families the boy's friends come from. Discuss your concerns with the other boys' parents. This may be sufficient to allow parents to join together to make a plan to help their sons.
- If you don't like what you hear, take some action to limit a boy's contact: forbid out-of-school contact.
- Discuss the activities that the other boys are performing. Draw out possible problems with these (see Chapter 5).

If you remain disturbed about the group your son is involved with, take direct action:

- Always ask your boy what he is doing, where he is going. Investigate the destinations.
- Enlist a boy in other, pro-social activities (for example, sport, volunteering, community activities).

- Be united, look for allies, others that the boy looks up to.

- Get further help, appeal to the school for a school-wide program (see below).

- Remove the boy from the influence of the undesirable peers. If necessary, change his school, forbid him to do certain things or go to certain places where he is able to continue contact with the 'wrong crowd'.

- Don't expect a teenager to accept limit setting without dispute. Be prepared to defend the actions taken, discussing why but not resiling from the fact that the limit is being set.

Doing Something about Anger and Violence Problems at School

Beyond helping an individual boy, many parents and teachers may wish to do something on a school-wide scale, because they perceive that there is a sub-culture of violence and aggression at the school. Nearly all government schools, and to a lesser extent many private schools, have difficulties with violence, and more can always be done about this problem.

A school's standard response to aggression in secondary schools is to suspend and expel. Expulsion is a disaster for a boy on an individual level: it marginalises him from mainstream education and drastically increases the risk of negative outcomes in maturity, such as poverty, unemployment, criminality, drug and alcohol abuse, and mental illness. On a societal level it is equally a disaster, as much money and effort is spent on rehabilitation of the unemployed, mentally ill, drug and alcohol abusers, and criminals. Every dollar spent on effective prevention is worth thousands saved by avoiding rehabilitation and incarceration.

Several methods are used to help violence in schools, which I summarise below. This is not a comprehensive nor a critical evaluation, merely a list that can prompt teachers and parents to do something, in accordance with their resources and energy.

School-wide Programs

These target every single member of a particular year level, or the whole school. They can include some of the following components:

Boys' development programs

Some schools have taken steps to establish development programs aimed at specific boys' issues such as sexuality, anger and violence, becoming a man and the like. Well-developed programs of this type do not exist in many schools in Australia but some schools have made significant starts on such approaches. The program content is typically broad and general, and it is usually conducted by enthusiastic and committed teachers, heads of welfare or the school counselling staff. The best programs are integrated into the school curriculum, and involve substantial weekly contact over a year or two. Shorter programs than this appear to have little effect. For such programs to work, they require committed individuals on the staff. Generally they have been developed within the culture of each school and do not conform to a general plan. These programs may also be useful in identifying boys who need further, specific help.

Peer mediation programs

Many schools have taken the step of implementing peer mediation programs, where senior and/or articulate members of the student body are trained to assist their fellow students to resolve disputes. Such an approach is an excellent way to remove the threat of coercive power from the situation, allow the warring parties to use words rather than fists or violent acting out to resolve conflicts and problems.

Anti-bullying programs

There are several school-wide anti-bullying programs that can be adapted to the needs of an individual school. Further information about these can be obtained from the Departments of Education in each state and territory.

Focused Programs

Other programs target high-risk students—boys who have shown some difficulties with anger and aggression and are at risk of suspension and expulsion. Secondary schools are ideal places to intervene with problems with anger and aggression. If a program is designed for early secondary school, this has several advantages:

- The most at-risk boys can be selected from the normal population of a mainstream school.

- Boys must attend school until 15 or 16 in Australia. Many may not be interested in academic subjects, and will attend a program if it is more enticing than mainstream classes.

- The program being located at school reduces the stigma many boys might feel if they had to attend a counsellor's, psychologist's or psychiatrist's office.

- Early secondary school is a time when problems are apparent, easily identifiable in the school context but prior (for the most part) to serious criminal offending. Early secondary school is the last time a program can be said to be preventative. After this time—mid-adolescence and beyond—boys normally face criminal sanctions if they are chronically violent.

Doing Anger Differently (DAD)

Some of the cases described in this book are drawn from my work in the DAD program, an innovative 10-week, 20-session course I have designed to help at-risk young adolescents deal with their anger and reduce their aggression. The program uses Latin American percussion instruments to engage boys into the process of group therapeutic treatment. The group therapy approach is described fully in the manual *Doing Anger Differently: A School Group Work Program for Angry and Aggressive Teenage Boys*, available through Melbourne University Publishing.

The DAD program has a three-pronged approach:

- It assists boys to discuss and question their experiences of anger and the influence of anger on action.

- It focuses on the formation of meaning and identity resulting from anger and aggression, in the manner described in Chapter 5.

- It emphasises group work with the interpersonal basis of anger.

The DAD program has been subjected to two research trials. These showed that, on average, boys who went through the DAD program reduced their participation in incidents of aggression at school to 20 per cent of the number of incidents of aggression they were involved in pre-DAD, and this improvement was maintained for nine months after the end of the program. This result appears to be amongst the most favourable of such programs.

Schools as a Unit of Intervention

It is possible, over time, to change the degree of aggression within a school by targeting the aggressive sub-culture at the school. One can conduct both generalist year-wide interventions, as well as specialist interventions for the at-risk boys. These can have the effect of lowering the overall level of violence within the school.

For example, I once conducted a series of DAD programs over 18 months, aimed at working with approximately sixty of the most aggressive boys in Years 7, 8 and 9 at a single school. The school also conducted a series of school-wide anti-violence and anti-bullying programs concurrently with the DAD programs. In addition, I organised a series of groups for the parents of those boys participating in the DAD program. The result, after two years of intervention, was a halving in the amount of aggressive misbehaviour reported by teachers the following year. Though this project consumed considerable resources, it demonstrated that it is possible to reduce the school-wide incidence of aggression and alter the violent culture of a school.

Appendix

Further Help

Sometimes a third party is helpful to resolve the difficulties that have developed at school and I have suggested in several places in this book when further help might be required. There are three principles you should follow when seeking assistance for your son:

- 'Try out' whoever you meet, to see if he or she offers an approach with your son that you are comfortable with. Don't be afraid to meet a few times before committing yourself.
- For an intervention to be successful, an adolescent has to wish to attend. Talk with your son to see if he would attend, or is at least prepared to give it a try. This can be quite difficult, as many boys are reluctant to see a counsellor, psychologist or psychiatrist. If he is initially reluctant, suggest a trial of three visits.
- Keep trying new professionals if you cannot find one you like.

In addition, several types of help are available. Which is most appropriate depends very much on the circumstances, and is best discussed with the treating professional.

Family Therapy

A family therapist works with whatever family members are willing and able to attend. In general, family therapy approaches rest on the premise that most childhood and adolescent problems have their genesis within the family and therefore the problem can be resolved within the family. Some adolescents feel most comfortable within this approach as they do not feel singled out as the cause of the problem. Though the treatment of an adolescent can never be separated from the family, working only with the family can put the adolescent at a disadvantage. It prevents him from articulating and developing his own views and ideas about the world, which may be something best done by an adolescent seeing a psychotherapist or psychoanalyst alone.

Individual Therapy or Counselling

Any individual therapy with an adolescent does not aim at arriving at a final solution to his problems, as solutions in adolescence are always a work in progress. An adolescent's life is so full of possibility that the therapy or counselling is directed towards ensuring the boy makes the most of his possibilities, forming and working towards his own goals and wishes. In order for it to work, the best approach should initially aim at understanding the situation from the boy's point of view.

Mentoring

Mentoring is where a more or less skilled and experienced person, normally at least a little older than the adolescent, regularly spends time with the boy. Such a relationship has positives and pitfalls. As I have stated earlier, the amount of time and effort required to assist a boy with anger difficulties is beyond what most mentors are able to sustain. If ongoing payment of the mentor is involved, it often results in a puzzling and confusing situation for the son: why are the parents not spending this time with their son but are paying someone else to do it?

However, mentoring has been shown to be effective in helping boys through some difficult, short-term transitions in their life, such as from school to work, or primary school to high school. In these situations, mentors can be a great help in stabilising a boy when he feels confused or uncertain.

Decoding the Helping Professions: Different Types of Professionals

Psychiatrists

Psychiatrists are medical doctors who are trained to diagnose mental illnesses and treat these, for the most part, via medication. Some psychiatrists are specially trained to treat adolescents and children and others are trained in psychotherapy, although these psychiatrists are in the minority.

Generally, no drugs have been demonstrated to have long-term effectiveness in the control of anger and aggression without having side effects. My advice is to consult a psychiatrist before allowing a young aggressive adolescent to be given medication, unless his aggression is occurring in the context of a well-established and debilitating mental disorder, such as psychosis or severe depression, or his aggression is such that it is causing irreversible damage to himself or others.

Psychologists

Psychologists have completed at least a four-year degree majoring in psychology and then have completed postgraduate training, either through on-the-job supervision or in a specialist course. Some psychologists specialise in treating adolescents. Psychologists tend to use Cognitive Behavioural Therapy, a short- to medium-term approach that treats anger as a symptom to be managed and reduced. Generally, a teenage boy can expect to learn a series of 'anger management skills' from a psychologist, to help him control his anger and aggression. The Australian Psychological Society has an online service to assist with finding a psychologist, at www.psychology.org.au.

Counsellors

Counsellors come from a wide variety of backgrounds and levels of experience. They are usually not as well trained as psychiatrists and psychologists—they are required to have only one year of training prior to gaining the title 'counsellor'. This lack of formal training can have advantages and disadvantages. Some counsellors have spent many years developing their skills and approaches with adolescents and are excellent practitioners, while others are undertrained and practise beyond their level of expertise. It would be best to avoid a counsellor unless some reputable agency has recommended one.

Public or Private?

As anyone familiar with the helping professions in Australia knows, there is a division in services between the public and private sectors. I describe the relative advantages and disadvantages of each.

Public Services: Child and Adolescent Mental Health Services (CAMHS)

All Australian states and territories fund public CAMHS, which are delivered in a variety of models and where professionals deliver services free of charge. Generally, there is a mix of family, individual and group therapy for adolescents.

The great advantage of CAMHS is that the service is free. The disadvantage is that although the level of service delivery is usually high, it can be variable. People who attend public clinics usually have no choice over who they end up seeing about their problems. In addition, CAMHS across the nation are underfunded and thus the amount of service that can be offered to anyone is also limited. If a family can afford to pay for private therapy this will be where they are directed.

Non-government Services

These are generally run by community-based, non-government organisations based in major towns and regional centres. The organisations often are aimed at young people and their families, and they will see boys with aggression and anger difficulties. One of the most prominent is the Reconnect program, funded by the federal department of Families, Community Services and Indigenous Affairs.

Private Services

A bewildering array of practitioners offers private services, the bulk of these practitioners being psychiatrists, psychologists and counsellors. Generally what is of most importance is the model of therapy used and the 'fit' or relationship with the practitioner.

Psychoanalysis

Psychoanalysis aims to help a person understand what his or her underlying wishes and motivations are, and then, if the patient wishes, to move him or her towards realising them. Many of Sigmund Freud's patients and those who followed him have been adolescents. As angry people focus on others at the expense of their own wishes and desires, psychoanalysis can be an excellent approach for adolescents with anger difficulties. It can be a method which sidesteps the problem of the 'blaming others' tendency of angry people. There are several psychoanalysts in Australia qualified to work with adolescents. If the ideas in this book interest you, then psychoanalytically oriented help may be an option to explore.

Narrative therapy

Narrative therapy is an approach originally developed at the Dulwich Centre in Adelaide as a treatment for adolescents and children with behavioural difficulties. Narrative therapy investigates the history of a problem like anger and aggression, and helps an adolescent try to imagine other ways of acting (much like the Cycle of Identity in Chapter 5).

Other

There are myriad other approaches. Generally, the best way to find a private therapist is by recommendation. Selecting a name at random from a directory gives little guarantee that you will find one best suited to help your son.

Notes

1. The Nature of Anger

Elements of my argument in this chapter are influenced by some of Jacques Lacan's early writings, in particular 'The Mirror Stage as Formative of the Function of the I' and 'Aggressivity in Psychoanalysis', both of which can be found in J Lacan, *Ecrits: A Selection* (trans: A Sheridan), Norton, New York, 1977.

The formulation of anger as 'I am not wrong about myself' came from an article by CT Warner, 'Anger and Similar Delusions', in R Harre (ed.), *The Social Construction of Emotions*, Blackwell, London, 1986, pp. 135–65.

The idea of a psychical danger comes initially from Sigmund Freud, discussion of which can be found in his article, 'Symptoms, Inhibitions and Anxiety', in S Freud, *The Standard Edition of the Complete Psychological Works of Sigmund Freud Vol. XX*, (trans. J Strachey), Hogarth, London, 1959.

2. Aggression, Anger and Ethics

Sub-types of aggression are defined in more detail in DF Connor, *Aggression and Antisocial Behaviour in Children and Adolescents: Research and Treatment*, Guilford, New York, 2002.

The definition of aggression as an existential act is drawn directly from Jacques Lacan's first seminar: J Lacan, *The Seminar of Jacques Lacan Book I: Freud's Papers on Technique*, (ed. J-A Miller), Norton, New York, 1988.

I have adapted my argument about ethics and morals from (among other sources) Lacan's seventh seminar: J Lacan, *The Seminar of Jacques Lacan Book VII: The Ethics of Psychoanalysis* (ed. J-A Miller), Norton, New York, 1992.

3. The Family: Love, Hate and Anger

The ideas of separation in childhood and adolescence have been influenced to a large degree by Jacques Lacan's ideas laid out in his eleventh seminar: J Lacan, *The Seminar of Jacques Lacan Book XI: The Four Fundamental Concepts of Psychoanalysis* (ed. J-A Miller), Norton, New York, 1998.

The section on mothers, as well as the discussion about the relation between anger and sadness, owes much to my reading of Freud's article on 'Mourning and Melancholia', which can be found in S Freud, *The Standard Edition of the Complete Psychological Works of Sigmund Freud Vol. XIV* (trans. J Strachey), Hogarth, London, 1959.

4. The Age of Adolescence

For some of my ideas about the importance of groups and playing in adolescence I relied on R Gordon, 'Symbiosis in the Group: Group Therapy for Younger Adolescents', in FJ Azima & LH Richmond (eds), *Adolescent Group Psychotherapy*, International Universities Press, Madison, CT, 1989, pp. 43–51.

Sigmund Freud's article 'Group Psychology and the Analysis of the Ego' influenced my thinking about identification in groups. This article can be found in S Freud, *The Standard Edition of the Complete Psychological Works of Sigmund Freud Vol. XVIII*, (trans. J Strachey), Hogarth, London, 1959.

I gleaned some of my initial ideas about playing and reality in adolescent groups from DW Winicott's 1982 book *Playing and Reality*, Routledge, London.

The idea of adolescence as a critical turning point belongs to many articles and books. Some of the most useful references are as follows:

the idea of adolescence as being a time for development of a critical habit of mind in D Moshman, *Adolescent Psychological Development: Rationality, Morality and Identity*, Lawrence Erlbaum, Mahwah, NJ, 1999; the idea of adolescence as being one of the three epochs of human life, and a discussion of identity and identification, in an article by M Pujo, 'Adolescence and Discourse', in D Pereira (ed.), *Clinical Psychoanalysis: Papers of the Freudian School of Melbourne*, 18, The Freudian School of Melbourne, Melbourne, 1997, pp. 56–68.

5. The Cycle of Identity: Reaction, Reflection, Action

The section on antidotes to anger is an adaptation of themes from ST Hauser, JP Allen & E Golden, *Out of the Woods: Tales of Resilient Teens*, Harvard University Press, Cambridge, MA, 2006.

The cycle of identity is influenced by the work of narrative therapists based at the Dulwich Centre in Adelaide, South Australia. Some influential texts were by Michael White:

M White, 'Pseudo-encopresis: From Avalanche To Victory, From Vicious To Virtuous Cycles', *Family Systems Medicine*, 2, 1984, pp. 150–60.

M White & D Epston, *Literate Means to Therapeutic Ends*, Dulwich Centre Publications, Adelaide, 1989.

M White, 'Deconstruction and Therapy', in D Epston & M White (eds), *Experience, Contradiction, Narrative & Imagination: Selected Papers*, Dulwich Centre Publications, Adelaide, 1992, pp. 109–51.

Also influential in my thinking was an article by Susan Nicholson that gives a reading of White's ideas: S Nicholson, 'The Narrative Dance: A Practice Map for White's Therapy', *Australian and New Zealand Journal of Family Therapy*, 16, 1995, pp. 23–8.

Examples of the Socratic maieutic stance can be found in many of the Platonic dialogues, where Socrates assumes the stance of an intellectual midwife with his interlocutors. Some examples are *The Sophist*, *Meno* and *Gorgias*, although there are many others.

6. What Parents Can Do: Techniques for Intervening with an Angry Adolescent

The discussion about the use of crises of possibility owes much to a text by Bruce Fink: B Fink, *A Clinical Introduction to Lacanian Psychoanalysis: Theory and Technique*, Harvard University Press, Cambridge, MA, 1997.

7. What Adults Can Do: Principles for Intervening with an Adolescent

The idea of showing as well as telling also owes something to Fink's text: B Fink, *A Clinical Introduction to Lacanian Psychoanalysis: Theory and Technique*, Harvard University Press, Cambridge, MA, 1997.

8. Intervening with the School

The idea of schools as a unit of intervention owes much to the work of Professor Arthur Horne of the University of Georgia, who gave a presentation that included this topic at the 2nd International Conference on Child and Adolescent Mental Health in Brisbane, July 2002.

Index

Page numbers in italics refer to case histories

ability to act, sense of, 25, 120, 122–4, 129–30
'Acting Out', recognising, 183
action-reflection cycle, 46–7
adolescence: certainty and doubt, 105–6; 'childhood made manifest', 59; conflict in values, 78; developmental turning point, 78; family influence, 10–11, 40–1; friendship group, 68; peer group influence, 41, 79–89; puberty, 10–11, 51–2, 77, 78, 101–2; search for identity, 78; spheres of influence, 79; thought development, 92–5
adolescent: acting then thinking, 100–1; ambivalent relationship with parents, 60; capacity for reflection, 121–2; considers himself above the law, 18, 34, 178; constructing own legends, 55; critical habit of mind, 102–3, 104, 119, 125; cycle of identity, 124–47; difficulty accepting limits, 172; discussing emotions, 100–1, 119; 'Doing–Being', 46–9, 82–3, 101, 106, 118–19, 145, 146; and 'family romance', 51–2, 58, 69, 74, 75; identity development, 78, 97–100, 142; inclination towards mastery, xx, 44–5; learning through experience, 145; learning to be a 'real man', 35–6; listening to himself, 118; meaning-making, 124–36; paranoid habit of mind, 102–3, 119, 126; placing himself in the picture, 47; reflection on relationships, 121; secret life, 189–90; sense of ability to act, 25, 120, 122–4; separation from family of origin, 59, 64, 75; setting own rules, 33–4, 186–7; 'unselfing the self', 81–2
affection and intimacy, 184–6
aggression: when anger is unbearable, 23; bypassing speech, 23–5, 48–9, 64; and 'conscience', 42–4; and ethics, 20, 30–1, 40; group mentality, 211; 'if–then' thinking, 93–4; implied, 49; instrumental, 24, 25, 26; justifying, 31, 39–40; maintaining 'psychical homeostasis', 23, 26, 35, 39, 49;

Index

'other-focused', 37–8; physical response to physical arousal, 49; and puberty, 10–11; reflecting on cause, 6; reputation of, 20, 85, 134–5; at school, 204–8, 208–9, 217–18; and self-destructiveness, 16, 37, 188; spheres of influence, 79; and victim-hood, 133; and vulnerability, 133

Alan, *13–16*; external figures as conscience, 42–4; 'if–then' thinking, 92; lectured to, 183; need for reflection, 121; 'other-focused', 38; own rules above 'written law', 34, 178–9; reactive aggression, 24–5, 26; and relationships, 120, 121, 174; relativity in ethics, 96–7; remorse, 26; self-image threatened, 13–16, 58

alternate fathers, 89–92

ambivalence, 11–12, 60

Andrew, 72–3, 74

anger: all the world's a problem, 8–9; and ambivalence, 11–12; contagiousness of, 27–9; directed in or out, 15–16; displaced from cause, xx, 11, 13, 22, 25, 190; escalation of, 27, 169–70; feeling wronged, 7, 8, 9, 22, 27–8; 'if–then' thinking, 93–4; intimidating, 26–7; one-way ethics of, 20; other emotions accompany, 7, 9, 12, 16; paranoid habit of mind, 102–3; perception of wrong committed by another, 7, 22, 40, 105, 122, 137; protective emotional response, 7; psychological aggression, 26–7; raising problems, 20–2; reflecting on, 6, 29, 122; and relationships, 12–19, 22; sense of unfairness, 7; a temporary madness, 3; tip of the iceberg, 12, 160; turns friends into enemies, 102; when is it a problem?, xviii–xxi

anger, antidotes to: capacity for reflection, 26, 88, 120, 121–2; focus on relationships, 120, 121; sense of ability to act, 25, 120, 122–4

anger, parental intervention: principles, 173–95; raising problems, 20–1; techniques, 148–72

Anne, 38–9; as mother, 38–9, 72; mother in role of father, 70–2

Anthony, *190*

anti-bullying programs, 215–16

attacks on self, 16, 37, 43, 188

biases in 'seeing the world', 126

Biddulph, Steve, 35

Bly, Robert, 35

Bob, 83–4; membership of aggressive group, 86

boys' development programs in schools, 215

Bungo, 85, 86

Charles, *xi–xii*; constructive contemplation, 159–67; example of intervention, 148–67; identifying crisis of possibility, 170–1; making peace, 167–9; making plans, 172; preventing conflict spiralling, 169–70; recognising 'acting out', 183; turning crisis into questions, 149–59, 195

Index

children: development of thinking, 93; 'if–then' thinking, 92; internal family, 69; and prohibition, 95; recognising parents' faults, 74; 'wish-to-be', 55–6, 57, 58, 64
conscience, 42–4
constructive conflict intervention, 149–59
constructive contemplation, 159–67
contagiousness of anger, 27–9
coordinating inferences, 93
crisis of possibility, 37, 49, 148, 170–2, 180
critical habit of mind, 102–3, 104, 119, 125
cycle of blame, 208–9
cycle of identity, 124–47

Daniel, 61–2; dealing with loss of mother, 60–1, 63; and needs of others, 61–2; parental absence, 180–1; too much talk, 195
David, 38–9; mother in role of father, 70–2; no vision of future, 38–9; not listened to or noticed, 181–2
depression and sadness, 7, 9, 12, 16
description of events, eliciting, 128–9
displacement of anger, xx, 11, 13, 22, 25, 190
Doing Anger Differently model: creating uncertainty, 144; detailed and nuanced understandings, 144; development of mental competence, 144–5; moral development, 30, 145; placing into speech, 143–4; using 'Doing–Being', 145
Doing Anger Differently schools program, 216–17

'Doing–Being', 46–9, 82–3, 101, 106, 118–19, 145, 146
Douglas, 52–5; ability to act independently, 173; lost adolescence, 52–4, 55, 56, 58, 59, 91; search for a father, 54–5, 56, 57, 64; stabilising self-image, 58, 59

emotional containment, 138–9, 140–1
enjoyment, restructuring, 193–4
ethics: and aggression, 20, 30–1, 40; discussing, 135; enhancing existing views, 31–4; one-way, 20; of peer group, 97; of self-interest, 36–7; victim-hood justifies action, 40; *see also* rules, laws and limits
exceptional outcomes, 137–8, 140, 141–2, 184
exclusion as victimisation, 15
expulsion, 214
externalisation, 7, 8, 9, 22, 27–8

family: arguments within, xix–xx, 10, 11; influence wanes, 10–11, 40–1; mirroring function, 14; psychical separation from, 59
'family romance', 51–2, 58, 69, 74, 75
father: alternate fathers, 89–92; function of prohibition, 65, 192–3; means functioning in place of father, 59–60; rejection by son, 72–4; as role model, 64, 67–9; in role of mother, 59; and separation from family, 64, 75
father figures, 66–7, 70, 73, 204
feeling wronged, 7, 8, 9, 22, 27–8
forbidding, 65, 192–3
Freud, Sigmund, 51, 55, 74

Index

future, doubt and certainty about, 194–5

'Giant Hands', 32, 33, 97
'godfathers', 89–92
Graham, *191*; parents not working together, 191, 193
Greg, *66*; ability to act independently, 173; developing own world view, 189–90; direction from father figure, 66–7, 70, 73, 204; reflection, 175; relationship with teacher, 66, 175, 204; restructuring enjoyment, 163–4; substitute father, 73–4, 204; 'wish-to-be', 180

'had it coming to him', 40

'I am not wrong about myself', 14–15, 117
'I'll do what I like', 17–19
ideals, 194
identity: cycle of, 124–47; development, 78, 97–100, 142; trying out, 78, 98, 99, 107
'if–then' thinking, 92, 93–4
inclination towards mastery, xx, 44–5
inference-based thought, 93–5, 107
'intellectual midwives', 119–24, 146, 147
internal family of child, 69
intervention with adolescent: affection and intimacy, 184–6; using antidotes to anger, 173, 174–6; constant presence, 180–1; creating doubts, 194–5; 'crisis of possibility', identifying, 148, 170–1; forbidding, 192–3; knowing what a boy wants, 179–80; limits to talk, 195; listening to and noticing your son, 181–2; making plans, 172; obedience, 189–91; parents working together, 191–2; preventing conflict spiralling, 148, 169–70; principles of, 173–95; problem of lecturing, 182–3; raising problem later, 148; rebellion, 188–9; recognising 'Acting Out', 183; recognising differences in actions, 184; restructuring enjoyment, 193–4; rules and limits, 186–90; secret life, 189; showing as well as telling, 173, 176–9; turning crises into questions, 149
'it's everybody's fault', 130
'it's not fair', 131–2, 133, 135–6

Jeff, 68–9
John, *17–18, 112*; above the law, 18, 34, 178; creating doubts, 194–5; ethical and moral concerns, 30–1; external figures as conscience, 42–4; glorifying aggression, 84; 'I'll do what I like', 17–19; instrumental aggression, 24; outcomes, 112–16; and peer group, 18, 19, 41; felt persecuted and victimised, 19–20, 44; putting action into words, 127, 128; relationship with teacher, 174; reputation inescapable, 20, 113, 115, 203; self-image threatened, 58, 59; self-inclusion in rules, 114–15; talking with family, 116; violence and power, 113; what was left out of story?, 126–7; words not fists, 112–13

Index

kernel of truth, 164–6, 203

latent meanings, 143–4
lecturing adolescents, 147, 182–3
legends, constructing own, 55
letting go, 71, 72
listening to your son, 181–2
loss of mother (sudden) group discussion, 60–3

making peace, reading the signs, 167–9
Matthew, 42–3; attacking self-image, 59; conflict with teacher, 42–3; external figure as conscience, 43
meaning-making, 124–36
mirroring, 14–15, 117
morality: importance of principles to individuals, 97; justice and respect for rights, 96; learning to act ethically, 95–6; part of human relationships, 96; prohibition, 95
mother: afraid of sons, 5; both parents acting in position of, 198–9; father puts himself between mother and son, 64; father in role of mother, 59; letting go, 61, 62, 63–4, 71, 72; means functioning in place of mother, 59–60; in role of father, 70–2; sudden loss of, 60–3
mutual suspicion, 169–70

noticing efforts at emotional containment, 9, 138–9

obedience, 189–90
one-way ethics, 20

paranoid habit of mind, 102–3, 119, 126

parents: ambivalent relationship with son, 60; assisting separation, 58; balance between guiding and stepping back, 76; constant presence, 180–1; discussing wishes, goals and plans, 58; failure guaranteed, 74; influence in meaning-making, 130–1; as 'intellectual midwives', 119–24, 146, 147; intervening with angry son, 148–72; intervening over peer group, 42, 100, 211–14; intervening with school, 196–218; lecturing counter-productive, 147, 182–3; listening, xiv, 181–2; own past a guide, 70; recognising positive behaviour, 9, 124, 138–9, 140, 141–2, 184; relationship with own parents, 185; response to childhood needs, 55–6; roles in raising boys, 59–60; separated families, 185–6; setting rules and limitations, 104, 177, 186–7; showing goodwill, 168–9; staying involved, 29–30; stepping back from conflict, 29, 30, 137–9; substitute parents, 73; understanding underlying issues, 156; working together, 191–2; *see also* father; mother

peer group: aggressive, 83–9, 99–100; attraction of a rejected social group, 41, 88–9; confining development, 107, 108; dominant influence by Year 8, 41; effacing oneself for membership, 211; ethics of, 97; extending boy's self-perception, 108; family and peer values conflict, 78;

Index

and family influence, 41;
forbidding undesirable contacts,
42; importance of, 114, 212;
legitimise and share actions, 84;
and meaning-making, 130–1;
'mirroring' function, 14; parental
intervention, 42, 100, 211–14;
problem of anti-social group, xxi,
41, 108, 211–14; safety of 'play' in
a group, 83; shaking association
with, 41–2; standards of behaviour,
41; surviving as outsiders, 79–81;
'unselfing the self', 81–2
peer mediation programs, 215
performing-meaning, 136–41, 143–4
persecuted victim, 19–20
Peter, 72–3; substitute parental figure,
72–4
placing self in picture, 49
'politics of rules', 44
'poor-me' view of world, 8–9, 62, 63
predatory aggression, 24, 25, 26
proactive aggression, 24, 25, 26
pro-social behaviour, 35
'psychical homeostasis', 23, 26, 35,
39, 49
psychical separation from family, 59
psychological aggression, 26–7
puberty, 10–11, 51–2, 77, 78, 101–2
putting action into words, 127

reactive aggression, 24–5, 26, 93–4
'real men', 35–6
reasoning, 93
rebellion, 188–9
recognition of achievements, 136–7,
139
reflection, capacity for, 26, 88, 120,
121–2, 135–6, 137–8, 175–6

reflection on anger, 6, 29, 127; action-
reflection cycle, 46–7; capacity for,
26, 88, 120, 121–2; 'Doing–Being',
46–9, 82–3, 101, 106, 118–19,
145, 146
rejection of father, 72–4
remorse after aggression, 13, 16, 26
replacing certainty with doubt, 194–5
reputation for aggression, 20, 85, 113,
115, 134–5, 203
resentful atmosphere, 168–9
respect for society, 65
retributive thinking, 93–4
revisiting discussions, 172
rules, laws and limits: adolescent
setting his own, 33–4, 186–7;
authoritarianism ineffective,
187; difficulty accepting limits,
104, 172; finding freedom
within, 186–7; finding own way
of keeping, 32–3, 34, 37, 45–6,
45; 'Giant Hands', 32, 33, 97;
having something to lose by
transgressing, 39; negotiation,
187–8; obedience, 189–91;
parents' role in rule-setting
changes, 104; rebellion, 188–9;
and resentment, 187; secret life,
189; unilateral imposition, 45;
written law, 31–3, 34
Ryan, *123*; ability to act, 122, 123,
129–30; capacity for reflection,
122, 135–6, 137–8, 175–6;
exceptional outcome, 137–8,
140; meaning-making, 130–1;
relationship with teacher, 175–6;
short-term gains, 133–4; stepping
back from confrontation, 137–9,
140

Index

sadness and depression, 16
school: coping with reflects coping with society, 200; Doing Anger Differently program, 216–17; expulsion, 214; mediating between childhood and adulthood, 108; parents intervening with, 196–218; peer mediation programs, 215; planning improvement in behaviour, 210–11; programs targeting anger and violence, 214–18; reporting disruptive behaviour, 5–6; taking action with aggressive students, 204–8, 217–18
secret life, 189–90
self-destructiveness, 16, 37, 188
self-harm, 43
self-image: anger a statement of self-assertion, 14; 'mirroring' function of peer groups, 14; reaction when threatened, 13–16, 23, 58, 59
self-interest, ethics of, 36–7
self-responsibility, 104
separated families, 185–6
setting limits, 177
sexual maturity, 164
short-term gains, 133–4
showing as well as telling, 173, 176–9
socio-centric behaviour, 35
stepping back from conflict, 29, 30, 137–9
Steve, 206–7
substitute parents, 73

talking, limits to, 195
teachers: alternative father figures, 204–5; considering themselves above the law, 178; importance of relationship, 204–8; improving school behaviour, 210–14; listening to pupils, 205; taking action, 208–9
thought: and affect, 9–11; definition, 93; development, 92–5; inference-based, 93–5, 107; from inference-based to reasoning, 92, 107

unconscious inferences, 87
unfairness, perception of, 132
'unselfing the self', 81–2

victim-hood, 19–20; and exclusion, 15; justifies action, 40; perception of fuels aggression, 133; a problem of separation, 75; with unilateral imposition of rules, 45
vision of future, 38–9
vulnerability and aggression, 133

Wayne, *196–8*; argues to be an exception, 198; both parents take mother role, 198–9; parents side with against school, 197–8, 200
'wish-to-be', 55–6, 57, 58, 64, 179–80
wrongful accusation, 9
youth gang, 85–6, 100